6.9¢

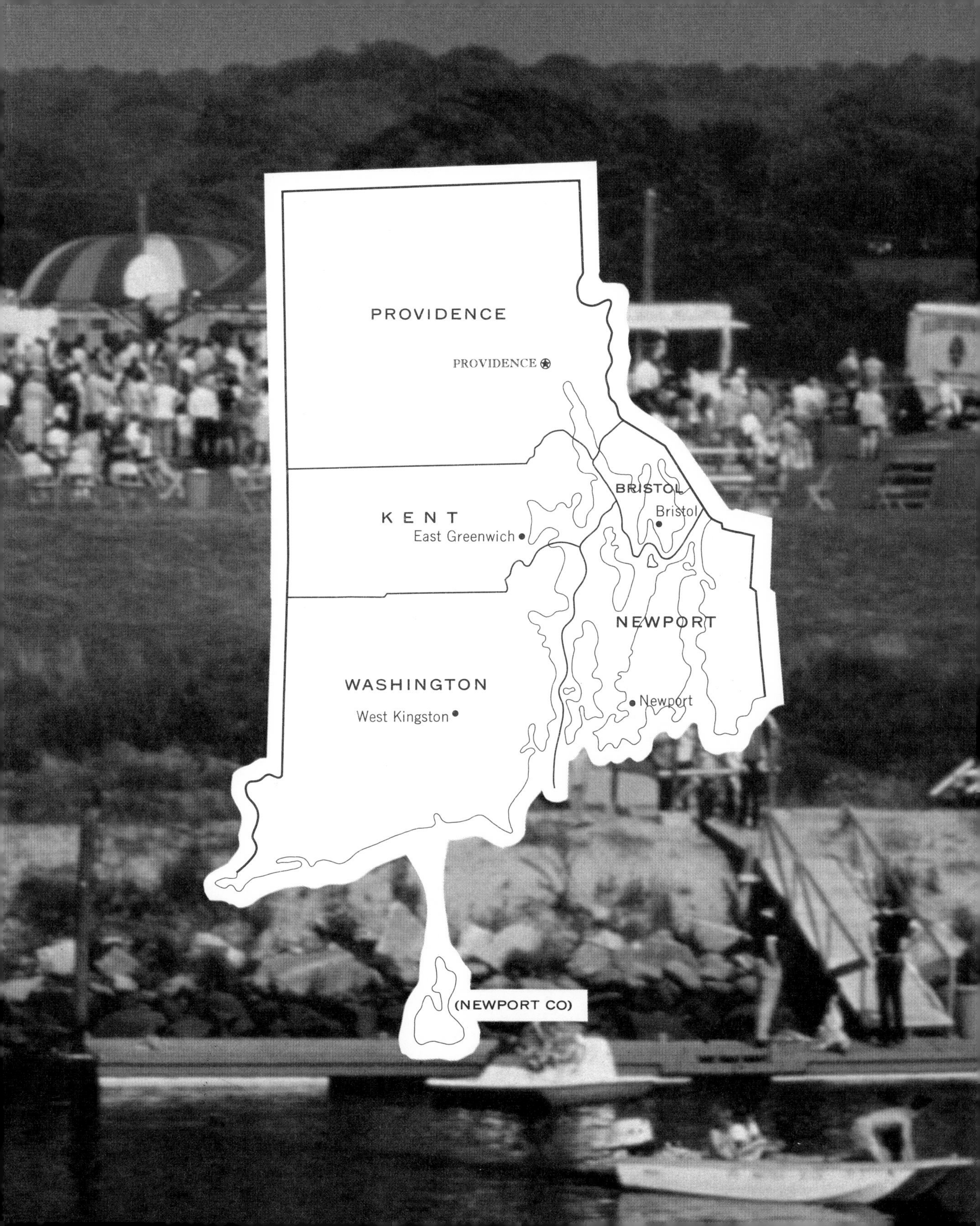

PROVIDENCE

PROVIDENCE ✪

KENT

East Greenwich •

BRISTOL

Bristol •

NEWPORT

WASHINGTON

West Kingston •

Newport •

(NEWPORT CO)

The New
Enchantment of America
RHODE ISLAND

By Allan Carpenter

 CHILDRENS PRESS, CHICAGO

ACKNOWLEDGMENTS

For assistance in the preparation of the revised edition, the author thanks:
CHESTER BROWNING, Audio-Visual Specialist and ROBERT E. WILCOX, both of the Rhode Island Department of Economic Development.

American Airlines—Anne Vitaliano, Director of Public Relations; *Capitol Historical Society,* Washington, D.C.; *Newberry Library,* Chicago, Dr. Lawrence Towner, Director; *Northwestern University Library,* Evanston, Illinois; *United Airlines*—John P. Grember, Manager of Special Promotions; Joseph P. Hopkins, Manager, News Bureau.

UNITED STATES GOVERNMENT AGENCIES: *Department of Agriculture*—Robert Hailstock, Jr., Photography Division, Office of Communication; Donald C. Schuhart, Information Division, Soil Conservation Service. *Army*—Doran Topolosky, Public Affairs Office, Chief of Engineers, Corps of Engineers. *Department of Interior*—Louis Churchville, Director of Communications; EROS Space Program—Phillis Wiepking, Community Affairs; Charles Withington, Geologist; Mrs. Ruth Herbert, Information Specialist; Bureau of Reclamation; National Park Service—Fred Bell and the individual sites; Fish and Wildlife Service—Bob Hines, Public Affairs Office. *Library of Congress*—Dr. Alan Fern, Director of the Department of Research; Sara Wallace, Director of Publications; Dr. Walter W. Ristow, Chief, Geography and Map Division; Herbert Sandborn, Exhibits Officer. *National Archives*—Dr. James B. Rhoads, Archivist of the United States; Albert Meisel, Assistant Archivist for Educational Programs; David Eggenberger, Publications Director; Bill Leary, Still Picture Reference; James Moore, Audio-Visual Archives. *United States Postal Service*—Herb Harris, Stamps Division.

For assistance in the preparation of the first edition, the author thanks:
Patrick F. McCarthy, Coordinator of Elementary Education, Department of Education, State of Rhode Island; Eleanore Bradford Monahon, Assistant Curator, Rhode Island Historical Society, Consultant in Rhode Island History; John H. Chafee, Governor of Rhode Island; Rhode Island Development Council; Greater Providence Chamber of Commerce; and *Providence Journal and Evening Bulletin.*

Illustrations on the preceding pages:
Cover photograph: Cliff Walk, Newport, Department of the Army, Corps of Engineers, New England Division
Page 1: Commemorative stamps of historic interest
Pages 2-3: Heritage Festival, Wakefield, Rhode Island Department of Economic Development, Division of Tourism
Page 3: (Map) USDI Geological Survey
Pages 4-5: Providence area, EROS Space Photo, USDI Geological Survey, EROS Data Center

Project Editor, Revised Edition,
  Joan Downing
Assistant Editor, Revised Edition,
  Mary Reidy

Library of Congress Cataloging in Publication Data

Carpenter, John Allan, 1917-
  Rhode Island.

  (His The new enchantment of America)
  Includes index.
  SUMMARY: A description of the smallest state, including its history, geography, resources, famous citizens, and places of interest to visit.
  1. Rhode Island—Juvenile literature.
[1. Rhode Island]   I. Title.
II. Series: Carpenter, John Allan, 1917-
The new enchantment of America.
F79.3.C3   1978   974.5   78-16446
ISBN 0-516-04139-8

2 3 4 5 6 7 8 9 10 11 12 R 85 84 83 82 81 80 79

Contents

The Slater Mill still stands at Pawtucket.

A True Story to Set the Scene

"FATHER OF AMERICAN MANUFACTURERS"

There was a clatter of wooden gears, a hum of bobbins, a whir of spinning reels. The medley of those sounds was music to their ears. Anxiously they looked at the twirling bobbins; yes, those bobbins actually were being filled with a soft, smooth yarn. The partners glanced at one another; the tension had been so great over the past months that they had scarcely managed a smile. Now broad smiles spread over their faces as they congratulated one another on their great success.

The story of that success is not only one of the most interesting of the many stories of enchantment of Rhode Island, but it is also the story of the first large-scale manufacturing in America—from this the United States went on to become the greatest industrial nation in the world.

That story started with a fourteen-year-old boy in Belper, Derbyshire, England, who signed an agreement to work for Jedediah Strutt as an apprentice for six and a half years, while learning the textile industry. That industry in England was just about as old as the boy, and Jedediah Strutt was one of the founders of the industry.

The boy was Samuel Slater, son of a wealthy yeoman farmer and landholder. Samuel had received a good education, and he had the energy and ability to be a very successful apprentice. He even spent his Sundays studying the machinery in the mill.

Toward the end of his apprenticeship, Slater began to consider his future. He had heard that wealthy Americans were trying unsuccessfully to set up textile factories such as those in England. To keep the manufacturing processes secret, English law prohibited any export of machinery; no models of machines or plans could be taken from the country. All mechanics were forbidden to leave England.

Samuel Slater decided to memorize every detail of the spinning machines and to go to America. Although they were not very complicated by modern standards, the carders and spinners were fantastically complex and difficult to memorize.

When he embarked on the tiresome and dangerous two-month voyage from England to America, Samuel Slater had to pretend to be a farmer. The only things he could take with him from the mills were his apprenticeship papers, and the proof of his six years of experience in textile manufacturing, and these had to be carefully hidden. If port officials had known he was a mechanic, he would have been subject to arrest.

Locked firmly in the young man's extraordinary mind were the most precious secrets of England's industrial revolution.

Slater started to work for a New York firm, but like all the others in America, the firm did not know how to make spinning machines that would produce yarn. Slater heard of a Moses Brown in Rhode Island who was trying to set up a textile plant, and he wrote: ". . . I was informed that you wanted a manager of cotton spinning, & c. in which business I flatter myself that I can give the greatest satisfactions in making machinery, making good yarn, either for stockings or twist . . . ."

Gentle Quaker Moses Brown replied, ". . . We are destitute for a person acquainted with water-frame spinning . . . if thou wilt come and do it . . . and have the credit . . . of perfecting the first water-mill in America, we shall be glad to engage thy care . . . ."

Slater and Brown agreed on terms for their first operation at Pawtucket; Slater was to receive a dollar a day and a partnership in the business. Of the expensive machines Brown had already bought, Slater said, "These will not do; they are good for nothing." So they started over again from the beginning, without any blueprints, depending entirely on Samuel Slater's remarkable memory.

At first, when the machines turned by Rhode Island's abundant waterpower were ready, they did not work. In spite of severe discouragement, the partners kept on and eventually they had the machinery going perfectly through the many processes for carding and spinning cotton into yarn. This yarn was sold and was woven by hand into stockings and other cotton goods. Samuel Slater was twenty-two when he built his first successful machine!

In the system of cotton spinning invented by Richard Arkwright in England, the cotton was prepared in the homes of various workers

Arkwright's system of spinning cotton.

by a system called flaking, which cleaned and fluffed the cotton and left it in large light "buntings." These were taken to the mill where the buntings were fed by hand into the mechanical carder reproduced by Slater from Arkwright's original designs. The various mechanisms of the carder straightened the fibers of the cotton, and these were pulled into a can in a continuous fluffy, ropelike piece. On drawing frames the sliver of cotton was pulled even finer and then made finer still on roving frames. Then it was wound on bobbins which were placed on spinning frames, where the yarn was drawn out to its final form and wound on other bobbins. From these bobbins it was reeled by machinery onto arms which made it into the finished skeins of yarn that were sold for weaving.

The firm of Almy, Brown and Slater was modestly successful. In 1793, they built a new mill, now preserved at Pawtucket as the Old Slater Mill Historic Site, and revered as the birthplace of the American textile industry.

Samuel Slater later went into business for himself and by extraordinary business management created a large personal fortune. During his first 20 years in America, Samuel Slater labored more than 16 hours a day. At one time in his thirteen textile plants he employed more people than any other firm in America. The Amoskeag, New Hampshire, mill, which he developed, later had more spindles than any other mill in the country. Slater's factory methods greatly influenced the economic growth of the country.

In addition, Samuel Slater helped his employees build good homes, established schools for their children, and is sometimes said to have established the first Sunday School in America.

In his later years Samuel Slater was visited by President Andrew Jackson, who was greatly impressed by the textile industry of Rhode Island. When the two men met, the president greeted Slater as the "Father of American Manufacturers." Jackson said, "I understand you have taught us how to spin, so as to rival Great Britain in her manufacture; you set all these thousands of spindles to work, which I have been delighted in viewing, and have made so many happy by a lucrative employment."

"Yes, Sir," Slater replied, "I suppose that I gave out the Psalm, and they have been singing the tune ever since."

Samuel Slater died on April 20, 1835, at the age of 67. His respected one-time partner, Moses Brown—also known as a founder of American industry—lived on until the age of 98. Samuel Slater left a large estate, and the family business was much expanded by his sons. The son Nelson lived for many years, and he and his father together rounded out almost a century of textile invention and management.

From the small beginnings of Slater and the Browns, who first set up a successful system of manufacture in the United States, the whole vast American industrial system was created, according to E.H. Cameron, Slater's biographer.

When Samuel Slater died, the Providence *Journal* asserted: "It has rarely fallen to the lot of any single individual to be made an instrument, under Providence, of so much and such widely diffused benefit to his fellow-men."

Lay of the Land

MINIATURE PORTRAIT

There is no denying that Rhode Island is the smallest of the states. It would take 483 Rhode Islands to cover Alaska.

You might think of Alaska as a great mural, and of Rhode Island as a miniature, an entirely different form of art, yet exquisite in its own way.

Rhode Island's area is 1,214 square miles (3,144 square kilometers). Bay and inland water take up nearly 25 percent of the state, leaving 1,058 square miles (2,740 square kilometers) of land. There are three main topographical divisions of the state: sand plain lowlands near the ocean and Narragansett Bay; higher rolling lands east of the bay; and the largest part, made up of higher land rising rather abruptly west of Providence.

At first glance, Rhode Island appears to have only two neighbor states. However, there is a Rhode Island boundary with New York in the ocean between Block Island and Long Island. Massachusetts encompasses Rhode Island on the north and east, and Connecticut provides a straight boundary on the west. Bristol County, Rhode Island, and Bristol County in Massachusetts are the only two counties in the country which have the same name and adjoin one another in two different states.

The state occupies slightly more than one degree of latitude, ranging from 41° and 18' to 42° 31' north latitude, and it is only "minutes" of longitude broad—extending between 71° 8' and 71° 53' west longitude. In miles, Rhode Island ranges 48 miles (77 kilometers) from north to south and 37 miles (60 kilometers) east to west.

The most outstanding feature of Rhode Island's geography is the huge wedge of Narragansett Bay, deeply splitting the state—a vast area of water large enough to hold all the navies of the world. Thanks to the bay and the many islands, the state has an impressive tidal high-water coastline of 384 miles (618 kilometers). The many branches of Narragansett Bay add to its variety; these include Bristol

An aerial view looking up Narragansett Bay.

and Wickford harbors, Greenwich Bay, Mount Hope Bay, and the drowned river valleys (estuaries) of the Providence, Seekonk, Sakonnet, Barrington, and Kickamuit rivers.

Little Narragansett Bay stands at the outlet of the Pawcatuck River.

The principal island of the state is the one that gives Rhode Island its name—the Island of Rhode Island, known to the Indians as Aquidneck Island. Next in size are Conanicut and Prudence islands. The state's great ocean island is Block Island, guarding the entrance to Long Island Sound. Altogether there are 36 islands within the territorial waters of Rhode Island, including such poetic names as Patience, Hope, and Rose islands, and such down-to-earth names as Hog and Goat.

14

The highest point in Rhode Island is Jerimoth Hill, rising to 812 feet (247 meters) west of North Foster, near the Connecticut line.

Napatree Point forms the southwesternmost extension of Rhode Island; it is the farthest continuation of a long line of barrier ridges of sand which separates the sea from inland ponds. Other pointed "extremities" of the state are Judith, Quonset, Sandy, Rumstick, Coggeshall, Coddington, Brenton, Easton, Sachuest, Common Fence, Fogland, and Sakonnet points.

On the political map, Rhode Island is divided into eight cities, five counties and 31 towns. In Rhode Island a "town" is the political subdivision which is generally known as a township in other states.

WATERS, FLOWING AND STATIONARY

The largest river to touch Rhode Island is the Blackstone, which has its source in Massachusetts and flows for about 40 miles (64 kilometers), entering Rhode Island at Woonsocket and cutting through both Woonsocket and Providence. The outlet of the Blackstone, which normally would retain the same name, has been given a separate name and is known as the Seekonk River; this is the drowned valley, or estuary, into which the Blackstone drains. Only about a third of the 540 square mile (1,399 square kilometers) drainage system of the Blackstone lies in Rhode Island.

The Pawtuxet River is the largest river flowing entirely within the state. It is about 28 miles (45 kilometers) long and forms a watershed of over 230 square miles (596 square kilometers). A strange river, related in its formation to a few other rivers that parallel the coast, such as the Indian River in Florida, is the Pettaquamscutt. Other large rivers include the Moshassuck and Potowomut; a smaller but important river is the Saugatuck.

Providence is probably the only city of the country that entirely possesses its namesake river. The older part of the city started where the Moshassuck and Woonasquatucket rivers joined to form the Providence River, which flows for its entire length through the city.

Rhode Island has only two boundary rivers. For about 10 miles

(16 kilometers) of its length the Pawcatuck divides Rhode Island and Connecticut. It has its source in Worden Pond and drains about 295 square miles (764 square kilometers). Of these, 233 square miles (603 square kilometers) are in Rhode Island. For about 2 miles (3 kilometers), the Barrington River forms a portion of the eastern boundary between Rhode Island and Massachusetts. This is probably one of the smallest state boundary rivers in the country and certainly one of the shortest of all river boundaries.

The largest natural body of water in Rhode Island is Worden Pond, which at one time was over twice as large as now, covering an area now filled by the Great Swamp. Considerably larger than Worden Pond is Scituate Reservoir, the largest freshwater body within Rhode Island. It was formed by damming the waters that joined to make the Pawtuxet River. The state is dotted with other reservoirs and natural ponds.

Even on the relatively small expanse of Block Island there are 365 freshwater ponds, one for every day in the year.

Another feature of Rhode Island water scenery is the salt pond. The barrier of sand that forms the outer ocean shore is often higher than the sandy land beyond. In many places on the coast, the sea has broken through this barrier and left bodies of water separated from the sea by a narrow sandbar. Some of these ponds are Winapaug, Quonochontaug, Ninigret, Green Hill, Easton, Nannaquaket, Nonquit, Quicksand, and Point Judith.

PREHISTORIC RHODE ISLAND

From the beginning of time, the surface of the earth has never ceased to change, and over the vast reaches of time countless interesting changes have occurred in the region of present-day Rhode Island. The rising and falling of the surface brought ancient seas and drained them away again. As this process went on, layers of sand and gravel and much plant life gathered, then were buried deeper and deeper until the pressures formed coal and similar materials, as well as sandstone.

16

Tremendous pressures beneath the surface folded and twisted great layers of rocks and then over the ages much of this was leveled by erosion.

Narragansett Bay is a part of a much larger valley-type formation created when the earth took a downward fold. This great "wrinkle" in the earth's surface is known as the Narragansett Basin and extends to Middleboro and Brockton in Massachusetts. Where the basin was below sea level, of course, it became the bay.

At some time in the remote past, liquid rocks from far below pushed their way upward and eventually hardened to form various types of granites. One of the most interesting of these is found at Iron Mine Hill. Nowhere else in the world does such a formation come to the surface. This granite is unusual because it is mixed with fragments of iron. Other evidences of the seething heat beneath the earth's surface are found in stones and rocks which are thought to be remainders of extremely ancient lava flows.

All of present Rhode Island was overwhelmed by the massive coverings of the ice age glaciers, some of them a mile (1.6 kilometers) thick. As these fantastic layers of solid ice crunched across Rhode Island on at least four separate occasions, they carved and sculptured the land much as it is found today.

As the glaciers moved south, they shoved ahead of them quantities of earth, boulders, sand, gravel, and other materials they picked up on the way. At their farthest advance they left these piles of material, known as glacial moraines. Block Island was formed by such a dumping process, as the edge of the glacier deposited the island material far out to sea, and then the glacier melted.

Some unusual bodies of water were formed by a different method of moraine deposit. In various places the largest chunks of ice took longer to melt. Sand and gravel in the ice melted out and was deposited all around the ice chunk, leaving round cup-shaped basins that later became ponds, such as Ponagansett, Lonsdale, and Hammond ponds. Other ponds were formed when the weight and force of the glacier carved out basins in the rock. When the glaciers departed, these rock basins were filled, to create such ponds as Stafford and Beach and Wallum Lake.

The Island of Rhode Island and some of the other islands in Narragansett Bay survived because their rocky formations were so tough the glaciers could not destroy them.

Another "legacy" of the glaciers was formed when the ice melted rather quickly and evenly over large areas and deposited widespread coverings of the sand which had been frozen in its interior. These are the sand plains still to be seen near Providence and Central Falls.

The animal life of prehistoric Rhode Island has left few reminders of its existence, but some of the deposits of petrified plants are especially fine. This is particularly true in the coal deposits. Mosses, ferns, and giant horsetails thrived in the climate of their time, and then were preserved when the rocks hardened. One club moss fossil found in the Narragansett Basin was probably 50 feet (15 meters) long and its trunk was 16 inches (41 centimeters) thick. This was found at McCormick sandstone quarry, East Providence. Not far away the dwarf descendants of this moss are found growing possibly 18 inches (46 centimeters) high.

When some pieces of shale are split, the tracery of seed ferns may be seen. These fossils were formed by the fern being pressed into the mud which later was compressed into shale. Some of the state's best plant fossils were found when a tunnel was cut through College Hill in 1914.

CLIMATE

The coastal location of Rhode Island and the great area of Narragansett Bay moderate the climate of the state. At times the warmer breezes blowing across the land in the summer and the blasts cooled by a continent of snow and ice in winter can be felt in the state. Quick and sometimes drastic changes are characteristic of Rhode Island weather. However, the Rhode Island Development Council hastens to assure everyone that Rhode Island never suffers the extremes of temperatures felt farther inland.

Block Island is especially well situated for weather. In summer its surrounding seas keep it cooler than the mainland, and the tem-

The sea provides many playgrounds for the people of Rhode Island.

perature never gets too high. When winter comes, however, the seas continue to moderate the weather, and winter temperatures stay warmer than the nearest mainland. Because of its situation on the Island of Rhode Island, Newport also gets much of the same relief from temperature extremes.

The average annual temperature for the state is 50.6 degrees Fahrenheit (10.3 degrees Celsius), with July temperatures averaging about 73 degrees Fahrenheit (22.8 degrees Celsius) and January, 30 degrees Fahrenheit (−1.1 degrees Celsius). Rainfall averages 43 inches (109 centimeters) and is fairly evenly distributed throughout the seasons, keeping the rivers flowing at about the same rate all during the year. The growing season begins about May 1 and ends around mid October.

During the 1720s, visitors from the Carolinas and the West Indies came to Rhode Island to enjoy its healthful climate and established the first resort in America.

Some Indian ceremonials have been preserved as public events.

Footsteps on the Land

PREHISTORIC AND INDIAN CULTURES

Few items have been found to indicate that there were many prehistoric peoples living in Rhode Island. This probably does not mean that people have not called the area home over periods of many centuries. It simply indicates that conditions were not right to preserve many relics of those early inhabitants.

One of the most important prehistoric finds was made in 1936 at the home of William T. Ide in East Providence, where a weapon point was discovered. Later this was found to be a Folsom point, named for the first stone weapon point of this type found at Folsom, New Mexico. This Folsom point indicates that prehistoric people lived in the Providence area at least as early as 12,000 B.C. Undoubtedly men lived in Rhode Island much before that time and for most of the time afterward.

When the region of present-day Rhode Island first became known to written history, there were five Indian groups occupying parts of the area. These were the Wampanoag, Niantic, Nipmuck, Pequot, and Narragansett. Of these the Narragansett were the strongest, although at one time the Wampanoags probably had been more numerous and more powerful. All five of the groups were a part of the great Algonquin language group.

The chiefs were known as *sachems*. These leaders had more control over their followers than in many other Indian clans. For the most part, the title of sachem was inherited by the previous sachem's heir. Lesser leaders, who ruled small portions of the clan, were known as *sagamores*. Unwritten laws and customs of the Indians were very strict. Serious crimes were severely punished. In the worst cases the sachem would perform the execution himself. He often personally attended to the whipping of lesser offenders. Land was held by the clan and the areas belonging to each group were well defined. A member of one group who killed a deer on the territory of another would hasten to send a part of the animal to the sachem of that group.

Indian children of the region were spoiled by their parents, almost never disciplined or punished; they grew up practically out of control and often were disobedient and insolent to their parents.

Among the more unusual Indian customs was that of the engagement and marriage. An Indian man would serenade his intended. If she threw her moccasin out to him, she showed interest, and then would come out for a walk with the suitor. Later the young man would display his "coups," the feathers and other symbols of his braver deeds. He would offer wampum and skins for a dowry. If the father and bride-to-be were pleased, all members of the tribe assembled for the wedding ceremony. This consisted of the couple standing together while the father wrapped the groom's blanket around both of them. Often a wedding feast followed.

Sometimes courtship was considerably less "formal." Less honorable braves would slip up to the houses of other groups, watch for an attractive girl, knock her unconscious, and carry her home as a bride.

Indians of the region recognized at least 38 different gods and deities. Most important of these was the great god Cowtantowit. It was from him that legend says the Indians received corn. A sacred crow brought one grain of corn and one bean from the garden of Cowtantowit, and all of those vegetables on earth have sprung from those two original seeds.

One of the most universal customs was that of the sweat bath. A small building would be plastered as tightly as possible with mud. Very hot stones were placed inside and water thrown on them to make steam. The Indians stayed inside as long as they could, then dashed outside to plunge into cold water.

When someone died, a kind of funeral director was called on, known as a mockuttasuit, usually an elder, a man of real dignity and sometimes of high position. The body was placed on a mat and buried with the mat and often with dishes or other possessions. Some possession of the dead person, such as a coat, was hung on a tree and allowed to remain there until it rotted away. The dead person's name was never spoken, and if a member of another group took the dead person's name, war was justified.

Often great sacrifices were offered in the name of the dead. Narragansett Sachem Cannonicus set fire to his house and everything in it as a sacrifice for his dead son. Sachems of the Narragansett were crowned on a rock on a farm in the present-day town of Charlestown. The strongest town and seat of Narragansett power was at what is now South Kingstown.

The Indians of the region had many rather remarkable skills. Many of the old men spent their time making beautiful cloaks out of turkey feathers. In colder weather everyone wore skin cloaks and other leather garments. Decorations in colors of blue, green, red, yellow, black, or white were often quite artistic.

The Indians never called their shelters by the term *wigwam;* their houses, generally portable arrangements of poles and skins, were known as *wetuomuck,* which meant "at home" or "at their home," and this term was changed into wigwam by the Europeans.

They used considerable skill in raising crops, and the women did all the work in agriculture except for growing tobacco, which was a "man's job." As many as 40 or 50 women might assemble in one field to get it ready for planting.

Fishing nets and baskets were woven, sometimes with great skill; clay pottery was made, although often rather crudely; and canoes

Indian Church at Narragansett.

were formed from logs by chipping and by burning out the center to hollow the logs. Although it is not generally known that the Indians used sails, simple sails sometimes were raised on canoes in this area.

Indian money, known as *wampum,* was cut out from the inner parts of shells and carved into coins which were usually strung like beads. The periwinkle shell was gathered in the summer to make white wampum, and the round clam shell known as quahaug provided a part for black wampum. Early Europeans came to use wampum for money almost as extensively as the Indians did. It is interesting to note that the black wampum was sometimes counterfeited from black stones.

Pans and pots were carved from soapstone, which came from quarries such as the one near Olneyville Square. This was a soft stone which could be worked easily and did not crack in the heat. A kind of throne was carved into the rock in this quarry, and it is thought this was used by the sachem as he directed the workers.

Today, the life of the Indians, who once may have numbered as many as 30,000 in the area, is remembered mainly through the many names of towns, rivers, ponds, and other geographical references. Possibly more of such names are used in Rhode Island than in any other state. The word *woonsocket* meant "at the very steep hill"; *quonset* meant "a point"; *pawtucket,* "at the falls"; *sakonnet,* "place of black geese"; *chepachet,* "devil's bog" or "place where stream divides"; *quidnick,* "place at the end of the hill"; and *shannock,* "morning star" or "squirrel."

"HALLY STRAYS," EARLY EXPLORERS

Did a Viking boat one day, a thousand or more years ago, approach the shore of the bay not far from Town Beach Road in Bristol? Did the crew jump onto a flat rock and go off to explore, leaving one man on guard? Did that man idly carve a picture of the boat and a few unknown words on the rock? Probably no one will ever know, but the legend of the Norsemen in New England has been heard for generations. New discoveries prove that early Viking

*The "Viking" mill
still stands
at Newport.*

exploration of North America was almost certain, but just where they may have landed, if they did, is still unknown.

Professor Wilfred H. Munro claimed to have translated the Bristol carving from the ancient Viking tongue and he said that it read "Hally strays himself and is lost here." Portuguese residents of Bristol claim the rock was carved by the Portuguese explorer Cortereal, possibly even before Columbus' voyage.

Even more exciting and controversial has been the "Old Stone Mill" at Newport. Promoters of the theory of Norse exploration have claimed that this ruined building was a church built by the Vikings about the year 1008. Henry Wadsworth Longfellow heard of a skeleton being dug up in Massachusetts, not too far from the mill, the bones still encased in a suit of rusted armor. He wrote his poem *The Skeleton in Armor,* associating the skeleton with the old stone building at Newport and with the Norse legends. At present the old building is thought to have been a mill built in early days of Rhode Island settlement—not a Viking relic.

Miguel Cortereal is actually thought to have touched the coast of Rhode Island as early as 1502, but the earliest recorded European visitor to Rhode Island shores was Giovanni de Verrazano of Florence, who sailed for the King of France, and visited Narragansett Bay in 1524. In the first-known written description of Rhode

25

Island, Verrazano wrote that one of the islands in the vicinity of Narragansett Bay appeared to resemble the Island of Rhodes in the Mediterranean. This may have been present Block Island. In any event, the remote and almost unknown Florentine navigator was the first to apply the name that later was given to the whole state.

Almost certainly large numbers of explorers, fishermen, and traders from Europe visited Rhode Island in the years that followed, but few if any records are found concerning their visits. Almost a hundred years after Verrazano, Dutch Captain Adriaen Block visited the island which has been given his name. The numerous Indians of the island received Block and his men with great kindness and hospitality, feasting them with fish, clams, game, and great quantities of succotash and hominy. Block also explored the mainland shore, called the present Pawcatuck the East River, and described Napatree Point: "a crooked point, in the shape of a sickle."

FIRST STIRRINGS

Children would hurry forward to greet the old man on his strange mount. He reached into his pockets and gave them apples, and then urged his ungainly beast onward. At least that is the tradition about Rhode Island's eccentric first settler—William Blackstone. Blackstone came from England to the site of Boston in 1623. After Boston was founded in 1630, the region became too "crowded" for his almost hermitlike taste, and William Blackstone moved out in 1635, settling at present-day Valley Falls, which was then considered part of Massachusetts but now is in Rhode Island.

William Blackstone lived in America for 52 years and died in Rhode Island in 1675. He was an ordained minister of the Episcopal church and a graduate of Cambridge University. He is said to have planted the first apple orchards in both Massachusetts and Rhode Island and legend says that he kept his pocket full of apples and gave them to the children he met as he rode about on his cream-colored bull.

William Blackstone was an interesting personality, but he took no

26

part in the actual founding of Rhode Island. That was left to one of the best-known names of early American history—Roger Williams. Williams had come from England to the Puritan colony of Boston in 1631, then lived both in Plymouth and Salem. He disagreed with the power of the church in civil matters and asserted that the king of England had no authority to give away land owned by the Indians.

Roger Williams' quarrel with the authorities grew until he was banished from the Massachusetts colony and fled in January, 1636, just before he was to be arrested for preaching "seditious" doctrines. He had become acquainted with Massasoit and Cannonicus, the sachems of the Wampanoag and Narragansett, and he first visited Massasoit, then went on to East Providence, where he lived for a time and was joined by five other settlers. However, they later found that his land was claimed by Plymouth Colony, and Williams decided to move on.

"GOD'S MERCIFUL PROVIDENCE"

The story is told that he paddled his canoe down the Seekonk River until he saw an Indian on the west bank who waved and called "What cheer, *Netop* (friend)." Tradition says that Williams landed on the rock where the friendly Indian was standing. However, Williams probably only answered with a wave and greeting and paddled on, finally turning up the Providence River to the place where it is formed by the Moshassuck and Woonasquatucket rivers. Here, refreshed by a freely flowing spring, Roger Williams founded what was to become the city of Providence and the state of Rhode Island.

He later wrote, "Having a sense of God's merciful providence unto me called this place Providence, I desired it might be for a shelter for persons distressed for conscience."

Because he was trusted by the Indians and knew their language, Williams was able to persuade them to make him a grant of land which was authorized by Cannonicus and Miantonomi, sachems of the Narragansett. The grant covered "the lands and meadows along the two fresh rivers called Moshassuck and Woonasquatucket." This grant developed as a typical plantation of the English style. By the fall of 1638, twelve other settlers had come to be associated with Williams in the new settlement, and they called themselves "the Proprietors' Company for Providence Plantations."

Government was extremely simple, with family heads meeting every two weeks to decide on any matters that had come up. A plantation covenant, similar to the Mayflower Compact of the Pilgrims, had been drawn up earlier; there were no courts or police. In 1640 a board of governors was set up, known as the disposers, to administer the growing affairs of the plantation.

One of Williams' many interesting activities was the founding in 1637 of a trading post south of present Quonset Point, where goods were exchanged with the Indians. He later sold this to finance his second journey to England.

One of the most important events of the early period occurred in March, 1639, when Roger Williams, Ezekiel Holliman, and ten others established the first Baptist church organization in America. Holliman baptized Williams in America's first immersion ceremony, and Williams then baptized Holliman and the others.

OTHER SETTLEMENTS

As Providence continued its growth, John Clarke and William Coddington (both from Massachusetts) came to Williams and asked his advice on setting up a new community. He recommended that they secure from the Indians the rights to Aquidneck Island (Island of Rhode Island), which they did, and in April, 1638, they founded Pocasset, later called Portsmouth.

In the next year Mrs. Anne Hutchinson and a number of her followers came to Portsmouth, fleeing from religious persecution in Massachusetts. Mrs. Hutchinson's influence soon grew so strong that Coddington left Portsmouth. In May, 1639, he began what was to become the city of Newport. Later the two towns united and formed a kind of "federal" government with Coddington as governor. In 1644 the general court passed an ordinance changing the

28

name of Aquidneck to the Isle of Rhodes, or Rhode Island, the first official use of the term Rhode Island.

Samuel Gorton came to Massachusetts in 1636. He was constantly involved in arguments with the authorities. In one of these disputes he was punished because he tried to defend his maid who had been reprimanded for smiling in church. Finally he was expelled from Massachusetts and fled to Providence but could not get along there either. He bought land at Shawomet from Narragansett Sachem Miantonomi. With Gorton were a number of followers who were as opposed to authority as he. Later the Indians said the agreement was not legal; when Gorton refused to go to Massachusetts to settle the matter, the authorities sent a force of 40 men to bring him back. There he was almost sentenced to death for blasphemy, but later was merely exiled once again. The community he founded in Rhode Island became Warwick.

INCORPORATION OF PROVIDENCE PLANTATIONS

The early history of Rhode Island is that of those four separate towns—Providence, Portsmouth, Newport, and Warwick—governing themselves separately. Then in 1643 Roger Williams went to England to get a charter for the colony, which was granted by Parliament and brought back by Williams. This document called for "The Incorporation of Providence Plantations in Narragansett Bay in New England." Under this charter the colony was governed by a general assembly with John Coggeshall as first president. Newport, as the largest town, had the greatest influence.

Roger Williams made a second trip to England in 1651. Returning in 1654 he became president of the united communities, a position he held until 1657. Rhode Island obtained a new charter from the king of England in 1663. This was the basic law of Rhode Island for 180 years. Among its statements was its goal to "hold forth a lively experiment that a most flourishing civil state may stand and best be maintained with full liberty in religious concernments . . . and every person . . . enjoye his own judgments and consciences."

DEVASTATIONS OF WAR

Much of the history of Rhode Island in the period which followed was dominated by war. From 1652 until the Revolutionary War ended, Rhode Island had a part in nine wars. Among the most difficult and costly of these were struggles with the Indians.

As early as 1637 the neighboring Pequot Indians had been almost wiped out by Connecticut settlers, and Roger Williams had made a treaty of defense with the Narragansett for protection at that time.

The worst of the Indian wars began in 1675 when the Indians of New England rose up almost spontaneously with a goal of driving the Europeans entirely from the land. The principal leader in this war was Chief Metacom of the Wampanoag group, better known by his

Above: "Great Swamp Fight" memorial.
Right: King Philip, a portrait
painted by Charles de wolf Brownell.

English name of King Philip. Another leader in the fight was the Narragansett Sachem Canonchet, who was captured and executed in 1676.

In this costly and relentless war to the death, almost every community in New England suffered some destruction. Pawtucket and Warwick were virtually destroyed. Twenty-nine of the seventy-five houses of Providence were burned, including the home of Roger Williams. The town clerk's home was also burned, but the clerk, John Smith, threw his records into the millrace. Fished out later and dried, all but 85 pages were saved, and they are still kept in Providence city hall.

In Rhode Island the worst battle of King Philip's War was the Great Swamp Fight, which took place in South Kingstown, December 19, 1675. There the Narragansett were badly defeated.

Captain Benjamin Church, who had a house near Sakonnet Point, was responsible for the death of King Philip. Captain Church had made a treaty of friendship with the Princess Awashonks, sachem of the Sughkonet, a very beloved Indian ruler. She furnished braves for the forces of Captain Church, and it was her men who finally captured King Philip at Mt. Hope, Bristol. Captain Church himself wrote a graphic description of the scene:

"So some of Captain Church's Indians took hold of him (Philip) by his stockings, and some by his small breeches, being otherwise naked, and drew him through the mud to the upland; and a doleful, great naked, dirty beast he looked like. Captain Church then said, forasmuch as he had caused many an Englishman's body to be unburied, and to rot above the ground, that not one of his bones should be buried. And calling his old Indian executioner, bid him behead and quarter him . . . . Philip having one very remarkable hand, being much scarred, occasioned by the splitting of a pistol in it formerly, Captain Church gave the head and that hand to Alderman, the Indian who shot him to show to such gentlemen as would bestow gratuities upon him; and accordingly he got many a penny for it." The execution of Philip took place on August 12, 1676.

Although Indian attacks continued for some time, the Indian power in the area had been broken.

THE PACE QUICKENS

King James II voided the Rhode Island charter and placed the colony under the newly formed Dominion of New England, governed by Sir Edmund Andros. Andros came to Newport demanding that the charter be surrendered to him, but Governor Walter Clarke sent the document to his brother, who hid it, and the prized charter never was given up. The dominion experiment failed within two years and England made a ruling that the charter of 1663 was still the governing force in Rhode Island.

Rhode Island experienced the problems of King William's War, the first of the continuing wars with France from 1689 to 1697. In July, 1689, French privateers, under William Trimming, attacked Block Island. These were private ships under contract to help the French. Reverend Samuel Niles witnessed the attack and wrote: ". . . they continued about a week on the island, plundering houses, stripping the people of their clothing, ripping up the beds, throwing out the feathers, and carrying away the ticking." Two ships were hurriedly fitted out at Newport and caught up with the privateers in Long Island Sound, where they killed Trimming.

To combat enemy privateers, the assembly of Rhode Island authorized privateers from the colony to search out and capture French shipping and naval vessels. Privateering was so profitable that when their commissions expired, many privateers simply turned pirate, and joined the growing number of pirates who were terrorizing the entire coast of the colonies. Even the famed Captain Kidd is said to have visited parts of Rhode Island from time to time.

Finally piracy became so bad that the Rhode Island colony had to take strong measures; twenty-six pirates were captured and hanged in July, 1732, at Gravelly Point in Newport. They were buried between high and low water lines, so that their graves could never be marked or remembered.

King William's War dragged on until 1697. After only a few years of peace, another war with France began in 1702 and went on until 1713. This was known as Queen Anne's War. Rhode Island furnished men and taxes to help fight this war, and privateers again went out. One of the most successful of these was Newport Captain William Wanton, who captured three fine French ships in the Gulf of St. Lawrence.

Rhode Island ship owners and captains were gaining experience which was soon to be helpful in an unsavory but profitable type of commerce. This was known as the Triangular Trade, because it involved a three-sided exchange of "products." Ships went out from Newport to Africa to obtain slaves. With the unfortunate captives in shackles in the ships' fetid holds, the captains made for the West Indies where they exchanged the slaves for sugar and molasses; this was brought back to Newport and made into rum. Fortunes made in this despicable commerce became the basis for the early wealth and society of Newport.

In 1728 the long-standing dispute with Connecticut over the boundary was settled. However, the continuing disagreement over the Massachusetts boundary was not finally settled until 1899.

In 1739 England took her colonies into a war with Spain, and this merged with the third war with France (King George's War). For this war the noted ship *Tartar* was built in Rhode Island and armed with 24 cannon. Rhode Islanders went halfway across the world to take part in various actions of this war. Captain Simeon Potter helped in attacks on French Guiana. Captain Daniel Fones led the *Tartar* in the attack and capture of the fortress of Louisburg in 1745. The French had invested the then unheard-of sum of $10,000,000 in this fort. About 650 Rhode Island men took part in this war.

The last of the wars with France (French and Indian War) began in 1754 and ended in 1763, and about 1,000 army and 1,500 navy men from Rhode Island served in it.

PRELUDE TO REVOLUTION

At this time, when the French were finally driven from the continent, peace appeared to be assured. Agriculture, the arts, business, and commerce began to flourish. Even science held the attention of some of the people of Rhode Island. One of the remarkable scientific accomplishments of the period was made by three Providence men, Joseph Brown, Jabez-Bowen, and Stephen Hopkins. Even with the crude astronomical instruments of the day they were able to observe the transit of the planet Venus in 1769.

In another field of accomplishment, Rhode Island "invented" the department store, when the first establishment of that type was opened. This was Gladding's of Providence, still doing business "At the Sign of the Bunch of Grapes."

Hopes for extended peace did not continue for long. As in the other colonies, the people of Rhode Island became increasingly discontented with the rule of Britain in the colonies. They felt they should be given more voice in any taxes they would be required to pay. The people of Rhode Island were especially concerned when the British government restricted the production of iron, hats, and woolen goods in the colonies. High duties placed on molasses, raw material for Rhode Island rum, also increased the dissatisfaction with the mother country.

Stephen Hopkins, ten times governor of Rhode Island, was one of the early leaders in encouraging the people to oppose Britain. Possibly the earliest action of any of the colonies against the British crown came on July 9, 1764, when Newporters and sailors from H.M.S. *Squirrel* fought with each other, and cutlasses, clubs, and stones were swung with bruising effect. Also, at Newport Harbor on June 4, 1765, American sailors were "impressed," that is kidnapped, and made to serve on British ships. Protesting this, about 500 sailors and young men of Newport captured a boat from the British ship *Maidstone,* dragged it through the streets and burned it.

As early as 1769 the people of Newport had burned the British ship *Liberty* when it brought two captured boats from Connecticut into Newport Harbor. Even more important was the "Gaspee Incident," which has been called the "Lexington of the Sea," and is often considered "the first open planned act of aggression against the British before the Revolution."

On June 9, 1772, the British sloop of war *Gaspee* was decoyed into going aground on a sandy point at Warwick, now known as Gaspee Point. At night, before she could be refloated, boatloads of men led

Burning of the British Revenue Cutter Gaspee *by Charles Brownell.*

by Samuel Whipple and John Brown rowed down from Providence, captured the sloop, wounded its commanding officer, and burned it at the water's edge.

Typical of the feeling of many Rhode Islanders concerning Britain was that of the people of Barrington, who in a town meeting sturdily opposed the acts of the British Parliament; they agreed not to buy any tea on which they considered the duty was illegal. If necessary, they determined to take up arms to defend themselves or their civil rights.

Providence was one of the many port cities across the colonies where a "tea party" was held. Most of these were held secretly at night with those taking part in disguise, but at Providence on March 2, 1775, a huge mound of captured tea was piled in Market Square, coated with tar, and burned publicly. A copy of a British official's speech was placed on top of the bonfire. One man went up Towne Street and crossed out the word tea from any shop signs he could find. Women who insisted on having their cup of tea generally did it in secret to avoid the wrath of their husbands.

Yesterday and Today

AN INDEPENDENT STATE

With battles flaring at Lexington and Concord in nearby Massachusetts in April, 1775, it became clear that war had arrived. Almost as soon as word reached Providence of the Battle of Lexington on April 19, 1,000 men were prepared to rush to Massachusetts to join the fight. Only two days afterward, the Rhode Island legislature met in special session and provided for 1,500 more troops to be enlisted. Governor Joseph Wanton was deposed from office on October 31 and replaced by the legislature with Nicholas Cooke, a Providence man.

"Two months before the thirteen colonies declared their independence from Great Britain, the members of the General Assembly of the Colony of Rhode Island declared their colony independent from the mother country. This bold and brave historic action occurred on May 4, 1776, and created the first free republic in the New World," as claimed proudly by the Rhode Island Development Council. Each year Rhode Island commemorates this milestone of American history with an elaborate celebration—Rhode Island Heritage Week, during the first week in May.

It should be noted that Rhode Island was never subjected to the authority of royal governors.

After the Rhode Island Declaration of Independence had been signed at the old statehouse, it was publicly read to the people of Providence assembled in Market Square. The reading took place on the balcony of Jabez Bowen's house where only 16 years before the people had acclaimed the new king, George III.

The name Rhode Island became official on July 18, 1776, with a resolution of the general assembly that "the style and title of this government . . . shall be the State of Rhode Island and Providence Plantations." Although this is still the official title, it is seldom used in full.

Opposite: Westminster Mall in Providence, a busy shopping area.

THE WAR IN RHODE ISLAND

The first naval battle of the war took place when Captain Abraham Whipple managed the capture of one of the armed boats of the British frigate *Rose* off Conanicut, on June 15, 1776.

James Wallace, commander of the *Rose,* approached Bristol in October and assaulted that city with cannon until he was persuaded to withdraw with the gift of 40 sheep. Because of Rhode Island's position of leadership in ships and shipping, the state's delegates in the Second Continental Congress persuaded the Congress to name Esek Hopkins commander-in-chief of the American navy.

On December 7, 1776, a British naval force commanded by Sir Peter Parker landed an army of 9,000 men at Middletown. That date was to become the anniversary of another attack on American forces 165 years later. On December 8, the British troops captured Newport and held it until October 25, 1779. Many Newport residents who were loyal to America fled to the mainland; the occupation of Newport proved to be one of the worst blows of the war to Rhode Island. Especially hard to take was the tyranny of the British commander General Richard Prescott. When his many regulations were not complied with instantly in his presence, he was likely to strike out at the victim with his cane.

Because of this, it was with great glee and much improved morale that Americans everywhere heard of one of the "boldest strokes" of the Revolution. Forty men under American Colonel William Barton, in five whaleboats, managed to make their way unobserved by the enemy down Narragansett Bay to the headquarters of General Prescott, Overing House. There they overpowered the sentry. A powerful black member of the party burst open the general's bedroom door with his head, and the startled general was captured in his nightclothes. They hardly had reached the boats with their captive before cannons and guns began firing. They made their way under the bow of one British warship and beneath the stern of another and got away to the safety of Warwick. An exchange of General Prescott later was made to secure the release of American General Charles Lee.

A replica of the Rose *can be seen at Newport.*

Bristol was seized by British forces on May 25, 1778. Alarmed by mistaken figures of the size of the attack, American forces withdrew without a fight, and the British burned almost 30 buildings, among them the Episcopal church at Bristol.

The heaviest fighting of the war in Rhode Island occurred on August 28 and 29, 1778, in what is known as the Battle of Rhode Island. Troops under General John Sullivan crossed over to the Island of Rhode Island from Tiverton on August 10; they managed to drive the British back to their fortifications at Newport. However, expected aid from the French fleet did not come, and General Sullivan retreated. The battle occurred during this retreat; neither side could claim a victory, but American forces were able to withdraw over the ferry and back to Tiverton. Some authorities believe that if the French had come to American aid at the time, the Revolution might have been ended quickly.

British forces were ordered to leave Newport in October of 1779; they took with them one of the town bells, books from the Redwood Library and the town records. When the boat carrying the records was sunk, a few of the records were saved and returned to Newport. By October 26, 1779, Newport had been retaken by American forces. French forces under Count Rochambeau, numbering 5,088, arrived

Modern soldiers reenact the Battle of Rhode Island.

at Newport on July 12, 1780. From that time onward, Rhode Island was not threatened by British forces.

Newport enjoyed the company of the French soldiers, especially the officers, many of whom were distinguished French aristocrats. The French were greatly charmed by the society of Newport and found the Newport girls as beautiful as those of the French court.

General George Washington, commander-in-chief of American forces, arrived at Newport on March 6, 1781, to confer with General Rochambeau. The French army gave him a full military greeting—one of the most awe-inspiring sights Newport had ever seen. As Washington stepped ashore, the French soldiers called out *"Vive l'Amerique; vive la France."* Washington was wearing the uniform of a marshal of France, signifying the authority given him by the French king to command the armies of France. Every house in Newport was lighted that night with candles provided by the public treasury and a grand ball was held in honor of Washington and Rochambeau.

A total of 11,701 men from Rhode Island enlisted in American services during the Revolutionary War. In addition to the commander-in-chief of the navy, Rhode Island provided the second in command to George Washington during the war—General Nathanael Greene.

At the time of the war's start, Rhode Island enjoyed the greatest production of iron and steel in the colonies, and this was invaluable in making the weapons of war. One of the country's largest manufacturers of cannon for the war was Hope Furnace.

All of Rhode Island paid a high price in suffering and lost resources because of the war. The toll was especially high at Newport, where, among other losses, there were 500 buildings destroyed. Hard times after the war lasted over a long period.

STATE OF THE UNION

Rhode Island was not represented in the constitutional convention of 1787, and the people of the state were greatly opposed to any outside "interference" with their business and trade. The national government made plans in 1789 to force Rhode Island into the Union, but did not carry them out. A convention in the Old Court House of South Kingstown failed to ratify the United States Constitution, but a new convention at Newport approved by a margin of only two votes, and on May 29, 1790, Rhode Island became a state, the last of the 13 original colonies to join the Union. Arthur Fenner was the first governor and his tenure was unique among all of America's first governors. He served 20 years until his death; later his son became governor. First United States senators from Rhode Island were Joseph Stanton Jr. and Theodore Foster.

The beginning of new industries and the growth of others, along with renewed commerce, followed. As trouble developed once more with Great Britain, Rhode Island was particularly disturbed because embargoes and other difficulties were disastrous to its trade. When war came, Rhode Island refused to allow the state militia to come under control of the Federal government. In spite of the opposition to the war, Rhode Island privateers such as Captain James De Wolfe of Bristol again made fortunes. Captain De Wolfe's ship *Yankee* at one time brought in a shipment of gold captured from the British. The story is told that De Wolfe emptied the gold on the floor. Lying down on it he is reported to have said, "I have always meant to roll in wealth." One hundred forty ships made Providence their home port in 1814.

The state continued its record of producing war goods. Providence's Franklin Foundry alone cast 60 cannon and Stephen Jencks produced 10,000 muskets at Central Falls.

During the war the British occupied Block Island, and there were many other alarms, such as the British naval vessel *Nimrod's* invasion of Narragansett Bay in May of 1814. Captain Oliver Hazard Perry of Rhode Island became one of the greatest heroes of the war. The state's opposition to the Federal government continued, but never resulted in an outright break.

One of the state's worst natural disasters was the Great Gale of 1815. Many Providence buildings were blown down, but the tower of the First Baptist Meeting House "wavered and bent to the blast, but it fell not.'' The tide was nearly 12 feet (4 meters) higher than usual; water rushed into the heart of the city; ships and buildings were swept away. Other ships were pushed into the city streets, and the bow of the *Ganges* crushed the third floor of a building on Market Square.

Steam navigation in Narragansett Bay between Providence and Newport began in 1817. In 1824 the Marquis de Lafayette, French hero of the American Revolution, visited Rhode Island and was enthusiastically received.

Also in 1824 a group of women weavers in Pawtucket went on strike. This is said to have been the first strike by women in the United States.

THE DORR REBELLION

Throughout the early period of statehood, Rhode Island's basic law was the ancient and out-of-date Charter of 1663. Changes had been proposed in 1797, 1811, 1820, 1821, and 1824, but those in power fought to retain the old laws and maintain their hold on government. A Constitutional party was formed in 1834, but a proposal for a new constitution was voted down in that year.

The main demands for reform were to extend the voting rights, to make the house of representatives more truly represent the people, to add a bill of rights to the basic law and take the courts from the control of the assembly. A "People's Constitution" of 1841 including these and many other advances was drawn up. The new constitution appeared to have been approved by popular vote, but the "Old Guard" declared the vote was not legal.

Under the leadership of Thomas Wilson Dorr, an election was held in which it was claimed that Dorr was the new governor. When he could not get the government of Rhode Island or the president of the United States to recognize his election, Dorr and his followers tried to seize the state government by force, but were defeated. Dorr fled to Connecticut. He tried an "invasion" in 1842, but was frustrated once again.

The state forces, known as the Law and Order party, called for a constitutional convention in 1842 (a new constitution was adopted, containing a bill of rights) and planned an independent court system, and other reforms. This was in effect a victory for Dorr, but his troubles continued. Dorr returned to Rhode Island, was convicted of treason and sentenced to hard labor; he served a year and was pardoned; he died in 1854.

CIVIL WAR

On May 18, 1652, Rhode Island enacted the first law against slavery in North America. However, this early opposition to slavery changed, and Rhode Island became the leading state in the slave trade, with great fortunes being made in this inhuman activity. The slave trade was forbidden in 1774, and a law of 1784 provided that slavery in Rhode Island would be eliminated by degrees.

The feeling against slavery grew strong in Rhode Island in the years that followed. The first of an increasing number of meetings against slavery was held at Providence on the fourth of July, 1833. The state joined with other New England states in the growing opposition to slavery.

When the Civil War came, young men flocked to the recruiting stations; the state quickly oversubscribed its quota and units began drilling. The First Rhode Island Regiment, commanded by Ambrose E. Burnside, was ready to leave for Washington on April 20, 1861, only three days after President Abraham Lincoln's call for troops. The regimental chaplain, Augustus Woodbury, described the scene: "The wharves, the heights upon the shores of the harbor and the coasts of Narragansett Bay were covered with spectators. Cannon belched forth its thunder. Cheers of men rent the air. As the steamer left the bay . . . the shores of Rhode Island had been left perhaps forever by the flower of her youth and the prime of her manhood."

The jaunty Rhode Island troops marched proudly through the streets of Washington and gave much reassurance to the citizens there.

One of the many Rhode Island heroes of the war was Governor William Sprague, who made a contribution of $100,000 to help outfit the First Regiment. He accompanied the regiment himself and took part in the early battles, having a horse shot from under him during the First Battle of Bull Run.

Six natives of Rhode Island rose to the rank of general during the war: Richard Arnold of Providence, descendant of Benedict Arnold; Silas Casey of East Greenwich; George Greene of Apponaug; Isaac Rodman of South Kingstown; Thomas Sherman of Newport; and Frank Wheaton of Providence. The most prominent from Rhode Island in the war was General Ambrose E. Burnside, who was not a native.

Of the more than 24,000 from Rhode Island who saw service during the Civil War, 255 died in combat and 1,265 from disease.

A MATURING STATE

Much of the history and progress of Rhode Island in the period following the Civil War was concerned with developments in manufacturing, transportation, communication, and education.

Among events of interest or importance was the equal rights act of 1866 which declared that "no person shall be excluded from any public school for reason of race or color." Rhode Island in 1874 became the first state to accept Decoration Day formally as a legal holiday. The first polo game in the United States was played in 1876, and President Rutherford B. Hayes boosted Rhode Island as a vacation state by enjoying one of the famous shore dinners at Rocky Point. After dinner he made history by talking over the newly invented telephone with officials at city hall in Providence, 8 miles (13 kilometers) away.

The first national tennis matches were held at Newport in 1881, and in an entirely different sphere, the 10-hour day was achieved by workers in Rhode Island in 1885. The nation's first torpedo boat, forerunner of the hard hitting types of today, was built in 1887 at the Herreshoff boat yard in Bristol and named the *Stiletto*.

In another first in sports, the first National Open Golf Championship was held at Newport in 1895. In that same year Cornelius Vanderbilt assured Newport's claim as social capital of America by completing his estate the Breakers, a private home never before equaled in America for luxury and elegance.

At the beginning of the Spanish-American War 2,300 men from Rhode Island applied for the state's 1,150 places in the volunteer army. Altogether, 3,246 from Rhode Island served in that short but bitter conflict.

National Lawn Tennis Museum and Hall of Fame in Newport.

With the return of peace in 1899, Newport was enjoying one of the first automobile parades ever attempted. A surprising total of 19 cars took part. Most of the society women gave pet names, such as Puff-Puff, to their autos.

An amendment to the state constitution in 1900 made Providence the single capital of the state, a position it had shared with Newport until that time. The state capitol at Providence had been completed in the same year.

The nation's first steam turbine for generating electricity was installed at Newport in 1903. In that year, also, wireless telegraphy was used to send news to Block Island. This may have been the world's first "radio newscast."

In the slow progress in the improvement of conditions of labor, the state's first workmen's compensation act, in 1912, was a milestone.

During World War I Rhode Island men and women in service totaled 28,817. Of these, 684 died.

A MODERN STATE

One of the worst textile strikes in the country's history began at Pawtucket in 1922 and spread throughout most of New England. The Rhode Island bureau of labor was formed in 1923.

One of the strangest events in the history of the legislature occurred in 1924. A Democratic governor was faced with a Republican majority in the legislature, and the Democrats decided to delay the passage of all appropriations until the Republicans would agree to changes in the state constitution. Before the matter was settled, there were even fist fights on the floor of the senate, and a stench bomb was placed under the chair of a senate leader. Banks had to loan the state money.

In 1929 the Rhode Island general assembly authorized the State Airport at Warwick, later renamed the Theodore Francis Green Airport—the first airport in the United States to be built and operated by a state government.

Above: The sunken Gardens at The Elms.
Below: The children's cottage at The Breakers.

The great depression that swept the country beginning in 1929 brought difficult times, but Rhode Island escaped much of the disaster. Only one brokerage firm, and no banks, failed in the state.

The first America's Cup race to be held at Newport was in 1930. In 1934 a Democratic majority in the state carried out a thorough reorganization of government. In 1935, under the leadership of Governor Theodore Francis Green, the state provided funds for the first free music performance ever given under the sponsorship of a state.

In 1936 Rhode Island celebrated the 300th anniversary of its founding by Roger Williams.

The worst natural disaster ever to strike Rhode Island came on September 21, 1938, when a hurricane and tidal wave swept over most of the state, killing 312 persons and causing $100,000,000 in damage. All of downtown Providence was flooded, some parts to a depth of 13 feet (4 meters). The high-water marks of the Great Storm of 1815 were exceeded. Across the state, almost 20,000 families were homeless or suffered severe loss.

World War II was heralded in an unusual way in Rhode Island. The *Westerly Sun* was the only newspaper in the country with a Sunday evening edition. Because the Japanese attack on Pearl Harbor came on Sunday, the *Sun* was the first regular newspaper in the country to carry news of the beginning of the war.

Another unusual distinction of Rhode Island during the war was to give to the world a new type of construction and a new word for most of the languages of the world. The Navy Seabees at Davisville near Quonset helped to develop the type of building which they called a quonset hut after the nearby Quonset Point. It was used with great success during the war and continues to be a popular form of building for a wide variety of uses.

During World War II, 92,027 men and women from Rhode Island saw service, and there were 1,458 casualties.

In the field of cultural activities, the Rhode Island Philharmonic Orchestra was founded in 1946. The first state-sponsored opera in the United States—the Rhode Island Opera Guild—began in 1959, and the State Ballet of Rhode Island is the only one of its kind.

49

The Breakers

Newport in 1953 was the scene of an event that now holds historic importance, although that was not recognized when John F. Kennedy and Jacqueline Bouvier were married in St. Mary's Church there. While Kennedy held the office of president of the United States, the summer White House was located at Newport.

On the 100th anniversary of its development, the famous Rhode Island Red chicken was made the state bird in 1954.

The next year the worst flood in the state's history swept across Rhode Island as part of the destruction of Hurricane Diane.

The election for governor in 1956 was contested because of the closeness of the vote. The matter was taken to the Supreme Court, which declared that the Rhode Island law concerning absentee and shut-in ballots was unconstitutional. The court decision reversed the result of the balloting in favor of Dennis J. Roberts.

In 1957 the flag of Rhode Island was the first flag of any state to fly over the South Pole when two Rhode Island men, serving in Antarctica during the Geophysical Year, took it with them on a flight over the pole. In that same year Rhode Island businessmen formed the Weekapaug Group to promote the economic advancement of the state. The nation's first state owned and operated Nuclear Science Center was approved by the voters in 1958, to be located at Fort Kearney, Narragansett.

The nation's first fully automated post office was dedicated and opened at Providence on October 20, 1960. The $20,000,000 facility occupies 132,000 square feet (341,879 square meters) in the West River Industrial Park. Providence proudly dedicated another improvement on August 13, 1965. This was Westminster Mall, which converted parts of the downtown area into a traffic-free shopping center, with landscaping and other attractions. In 1966 Governor John H. Chafee was reelected for a third term. Ten years later, in 1976, the state celebrated the national Bicentennial and welcomed the tall sailing ships.

THE PEOPLE OF RHODE ISLAND

"More ideas which have become national have emanated from the little colony of Rhode Island than from all American states," was the claim of eminent historian George Bancroft. Of all their ideas and contributions, perhaps Rhode Island people are rightfully most proud of the pioneering that they provided in the matter of religious freedom.

The state claims title of the "first free haven of religious worship in the New World," and, the colony's code of laws of 1647 declared, "all men may walk as their consciences persuade them, everyone in the name of his God." Rhode Island's early settlers were probably the most diversified and intelligent group of religious and political nonconformists ever gathered in one colony. These freethinking men established at Providence in 1639 the first Baptist congregation in the country. Other evidences of Rhode Island's religious tolerance are found at Newport, where stands the oldest Jewish synagogue in

*The interior of
Touro Synagogue
in Newport.*

America (1763) — the congregation dates back to 1658; and the oldest Quaker meeting house in the nation (1699). The Quakers first found refuge in Rhode Island in 1657. Roger Williams thought their religious ideas were incorrect, but he would have resisted any attempt to suppress them, and they were given a place in the colony's society.

In 1780, Roman Catholic masses in Rhode Island were first held in the Old Colony House in Newport by French chaplains of the army forces stationed there. Today over half of the population of Rhode Island is Catholic.

George Berkeley summed up the feeling of Rhode Island for religious toleration when he wrote to a friend in Ireland in 1729: "Here are four sorts of Anabaptists, besides, Presbyterians,

52

Quakers, Independents and many of no profession at all. Notwithstanding so many differences here are fewer quarrels about religion than elsewhere, the people living peaceable with their neighbors of whatsoever permission."

The diversified national background of Rhode Islanders was pointed up by Stuart Hale of the Providence *Journal-Bulletin:* "Take a staid, industrious Yankee town. Add a full measure of sturdy Italian stock and blend in liberal amounts from the Emerald Isle (remove the brogue, but slowly), sprinkle with honest Polish faces (leaving in the polkas), and the sons and daughters of French Canada. Spice with the products of Portugal, Greece, Armenia and other warm lands. Stir well and serve—that's Providence."

At the present time there are more people of Italian descent in Rhode Island than from any other ethnic group.

The second largest group is the French Canadian population. Woonsocket has sometimes been called "New Canada" and at one time it was estimated that 75 percent of the population of Woonsocket was of French-Canadian background.

There are less than 30,000 black residents in Rhode Island. Of the original population of the state—the Indians—less than 1,000 remain. Remnants of the Narragansett hold an annual reunion near Charlestown.

It has been said that the State of Rhode Island and Providence Plantations is the smallest state, with the longest name and the shortest motto: *Hope!* Since its very beginning it has held out that hope to the people of the world.

Rocky cliffs are found along the Atlantic Coast.
Here is the striking geography of Muhegan Bluffs.

Natural Treasures

Among the most notable of the natural resources of Rhode Island are the creatures of the sea. The world's best giant bluefin tuna fishing grounds have been found off the Southeast Lighthouse on Block Island. A record bluefin tuna caught on rod and reel was hooked off Natunuck in 1951. It weighed 961.5 pounds (436 kilograms). A world record swordfish was also caught in Rhode Island waters, a 900-pound (408-kilogram) monster snagged in 1952. Still another world record fish—the striped bass—was taken from the ocean off Rhode Island.

The world's largest organized deep-sea sports fishing competition is the annual United States Atlantic Tuna Tournament, held at Galilee near Narragansett Pier. The fleet of boats taking part in this averages 140, and there are often 150,000 spectators.

Other deep-sea prizes include white marlin, tautog, bluefish, snapper, mackerel, flounder, squeteague, pollock, and scup. The annual run of scup near Newport is eagerly awaited.

Those who think "fish ladders" are modern would be interested to know that as early as 1761 the general assembly authorized the running of a lottery in order to build "a passage around Pawtucket Falls so that fish of almost every kind, who choose fresh water at certain seasons of the year, may pass with ease."

The state's waters are also noted for the famous quahaug clam; oysters have been cultivated since before 1800, and the delicious blue crab and lobster are eagerly sought by those who like good eating. The state operates a lobster hatchery at Wickford.

Deer are the only large game animal now found in Rhode Island. Deer may be hunted by archers but only after they have obtained a "certificate of competency" in the use of this ancient type of weapon. All who stalk the deer with bow and arrow must take a free state course in archery. Several hundred pass this course each year. Other animals of the state are rabbits, other rodents, and similar small game common to most of the country.

Local bird lovers have recorded 358 species of birds within Rhode Island. Of these 196 come annually, while 162 have been found only on a few occasions. Among the more interesting birds have been the yellow flicker, pileated woodpecker, yellow throated warbler, great blue heron, albino blue jay, American egret, cedar waxwing, cardinal, tufted titmouse, mockingbird, evening grosbeak, tern, and wood duck. The wood duck almost became extinct but managed to make a comeback. Among the more "famous" Rhode Island birds must be listed the most northerly known colony of nesting cattle egrets in North America. There are 26 species of shore birds.

The most notable bird activity in the state is the annual migration of birds over Rhode Island, one of only two or three places in the country where similar numbers and kinds of migrating birds can be seen on certain days in May and October. A "river" of thousands of small birds flows above the landscape.

Many bird species are declining. The noble peregrine falcon has vanished from the region; the osprey has dwindled to only a few pairs in Rhode Island; the black-crowned night heron is much reduced, as are many others.

Due to the influence of Narragansett Bay, trees and flowers found in both the North and South thrive in Rhode Island. In this small state there are 60 different kinds of trees. The large numbers of flowers include 30 kinds of orchids alone, the blue gentian, the tall wild iris, the strange insect-eating pitcher plants, and the rare pink pond lilies.

Newcomers are surprised to find mountain laurel, rhododendron, and flowering dogwood in Rhode Island.

One of the interesting of the more modest forms of life is the eel grass, prized for making fertilizer.

Probably the best known of the state's minerals is the unique Rhode Island coal. It is compressed so hard that it almost refuses to burn. The poet William Cullen Bryant wrote *Meditation on Rhode Island Coal,* a humorous commentary on that unusual mineral.

Building stone—granite, limestone, and sandstone—is the most important type of mineral found in the state. The state's dark greenstone is particularly valued. The strange iron-bearing rock of Iron Mine Hill is found nowhere else in the world. Quartz, calcite, epidote, bowenite, and sand and gravel are other minerals.

People Use Their Treasures

WHERE INDUSTRY BEGAN

Rhode Island holds probably the proudest record of the entire country in the field of business and industry. In this tiny state, modern manufacturing in America—the great industrial revolution—was begun, a movement which was to make America the greatest manufacturing nation in the world.

When in 1790 the Blackstone River provided power for machines which in December, 1790, spun the first thread ever made by machine in America, it was a technical triumph—America's first cotton mill—but the output was small. However, by 1815 there were 100 mills in operation.

For a while the manufactured thread was still woven into cloth on looms at home; then large numbers of weavers were brought together in factories to weave cloth on hand looms. After 1815, power weaving looms and other water-driven machinery were introduced. Eventually the typical mill was fully mechanized for cleaning, carding, spinning, weaving, and finishing, though many still sent their cloth out for bleaching, dyeing, or printing. The great American textile industry was on its way.

The first woolen power looms in America were introduced by Rowland Hazard at Peace Dale in 1816. To encourage the woolen industry, President James Madison wore a suit of Pawtucket wool to his inauguration. Eventually Rhode Island became the greatest woolen center of the country. By 1890, Providence, Woonsocket, and Pawtucket formed the heart of the American woolen industry. Rhode Island is still the leading woolen manufacturing state.

In a highly specialized field of the textile industry, Rhode Island leads the country in fine lace making, producing more than half the lace made in the United States.

Rhode Island was also the birthplace of the great American jewelry industry. Nehemia Dodge of Providence devised a method of plating inexpensive metals with gold. Until this time only the rich could afford jewelry. Dodge manufactured his stock in advance and his customers could make their selections in his shop. In this manner he laid the foundation for modern jewelry making and sales practices.

In 1880 Rhode Island became first among all the states in jewelry production, a position which it has held to the present day. The state is sometimes called the costume jewelry center of the world.

Beautiful silver designs perpetuate the tradition of fine manufacturing craftsmanship.

Rhode Island is also the home of America's leading silversmiths. No other state has a similar concentration. A helper of Dodge, Jabez Gorham, began to make silver spoons and sell them house to house. This was the beginning of the vast Gorham Manufacturing Company, one of the world's largest silver producers. In 1886 a writer said, "The manufactory is one of the wonders of the country if not of the world." Rhode Island firms which manufacture jewelry or work with precious metals number nearly a thousand.

Today the primary metal trades industry follows textiles and jewelry and silverware in dollar value. The rubber and plastics industry holds fourth rank in the state.

Shipbuilding in Rhode Island began in the 1640s, and Narragansett Bay is still an important ship and yacht producing center.

Other important industries are food products, printing and publishing, instruments and optical goods, and apparel.

Among the state's many manufacturing distinctions is an unusual claim to fame. The California Artificial Flower Company of Providence is the largest manufacturer of artificial flowers in the world.

In proportion to its size, Rhode Island is considered the most highly industrialized state in the nation. Since 1939 it has had a larger percentage of its population employed in industry than any other state.

All industries in the state produce goods valued at nearly two billion dollars a year.

FROM SEA, SOIL, AND UNDERGROUND

Among Rhode Island's agricultural accomplishments might be listed "giving the modern poultry industry to the world." In 1854 Captain William Tripp of Little Compton and John Macomber of Westport, Massachusetts, began to cross Malay and Java roosters with hens from China. The resulting chickens were crossed with other breeds; these efforts finally led to the famous Rhode Island Red, which is noted both for large amounts of excellent meat and good egg laying. The people of Rhode Island are proud of their state

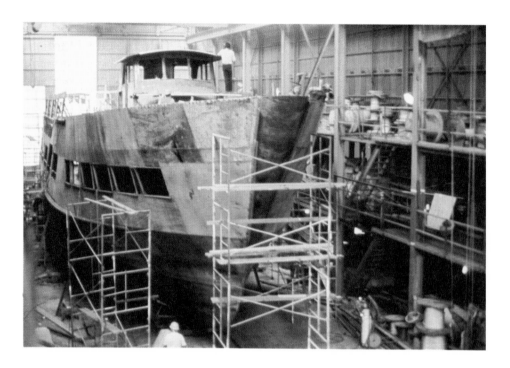

Shipbuilding at Blount Marine.

bird and the contribution it has made to world agriculture. Not so well known is the fact that there is also a Rhode Island White.

Rhode Island is also noted for developing another popular agricultural product, the greening apple.

Today's agriculture in Rhode Island is devoted mostly to truck gardening and dairying. Sweet corn, tomatoes, beans, cabbage, and squash all flourish in the favorable climate of the state. Potatoes are the oldest commercial crop, and over 4,000 acres (1,619 hectares) of potatoes produce revenue of about $6,000,000 per year. Nursery stock is another large item in Rhode Island agriculture.

The total farm income for Rhode Island averages about $50,000,-000. For a state so small and so highly industrialized this is really a remarkable figure. The contrast with giant Alaska's total of only over $4,000,000 agricultural income indicates the tremendous influence of weather and climate in farming.

Commercial fishing in Rhode Island brings in about $20,000,000 per year to the state. Large hauls of edible fish include bluefish, squid, cod, butterfish, sea bass, mackerel, scup, flounder, and pollack. Galilee is the main fisheries center. Non-edible fish are broken down for fish oil, fish meal, and other products. Lobster and shell fishermen also are active. Shellfish bring in almost half the value of commercial fisheries in Rhode Island.

The principal mineral industry of Rhode Island is the production of sand and gravel, followed by building stone. The quarry at Limerock is considered to be the oldest limestone quarry operating in the United States. It is generally thought that this was opened as early as 1643 by Thomas Harris. Mineral production in Rhode Island accounts for income of about $5,000,000 per year. Although 50th in size, Rhode Island ranks 49th in value of mineral production—ahead of Delaware.

TRANSPORTATION AND COMMUNICATION

Because of Narragansett Bay, shipping has been one of the earliest activities of Rhode Island. The first warehouse and wharf at Providence were built in 1680. Today the city is the third busiest port of New England. Its 42-foot (13-meter) deep channels can accommodate most of the world's ocean freighters.

Until the early 1800s Newport was the leading port of Rhode Island. Newport ships were known in almost every port of the world. Few Newport women were without carpets from Turkey, shawls from India, the silks of China, sandalwood boxes, monkeys, parrots, and other exotic items from everywhere.

Bristol was another leading port—at one time the fourth busiest in the country. Both Bristol and Newport had large whaling operations.

The first steam railroad operating in Rhode Island was the line that connected Boston and Providence in 1835, but only a small part of the line ran through Rhode Island. The main through line today is the New Haven Railroad, on the line between Boston and New York.

The port of Providence.

Beginning with Indian trails, the roads of Rhode Island have expanded to the present modern highway system. This is topped by the state's portion of the great Interstate system, including Interstates 95, 195, and 295 in Rhode Island.

Major airlines serve the Theodore Francis Green Airport at Hillsgrove in Warwick, the state's principal airline terminal.

The Rhode Island *Gazette* was the first newspaper published in the state; it began operation in 1732 but ceased only seven months later. This was established by the brother of Benjamin Franklin, James Franklin, who had fled from Massachusetts and set up Rhode Island's first printing press in 1727. In that same year he published *The Rhode Island Almanack* by Poor Robin. Franklin's son James established the Newport *Mercury* in 1758. The *Mercury,* in 1934, became a weekly edition of the Newport *News* and is now named the Newport *Mercury and News.*

Human Treasures

CREATIVE DISSENTER

Roger Williams was the first of America's three great founders of colonies, along with William Penn of Pennsylvania and James Oglethorpe of Georgia. Among all the thirteen colonies, only three were so indelibly impressed with the stamp of their originator that they are considered to have been "founded" by one man. Of the three, perhaps, Williams' claims to the title are the least strong, but history is undoubtedly correct in naming him one of the three founding fathers of American states.

Roger Williams was born in London in 1603. He graduated from Cambridge in 1626 and became a minister of the Church of England. He came to Massachusetts February 9, 1631, and almost immediately showed a talent for rubbing people the wrong way, which frequently made difficulty for him throughout his life. He felt strongly that the church had no right to control the government. Additionally, he disagreed on other church matters, and lost no opportunity to present his disagreements forcefully and sometimes with little tact. He also felt that the Indians' rights were being taken away from them.

If Roger Williams had not been banished in 1635, Rhode Island might have been taken over by one of the other colonies. The religious toleration in Rhode Island which served as such a fine example for the later Federal government of the United States might never have existed.

Roger Williams was a man whose views changed quickly on most matters except human freedom and dignity. He became a Baptist but soon decided that he did not believe in any one creed or church. He certainly deserved the title so often given him as "first champion of complete religious freedom in America."

On his two trips to England he not only worked for the good of his colony in America, but also published pamphlets giving his views opposing the established church and other matters. As a writer he also was the author of *A Key Into the Language of America,* one of the most understanding and authoritative works ever published on the Indian languages.

Roger Williams served three terms as president of Rhode Island (1654 to 1657). He lived until March 25, 1683, long enough to see the colony change from a wilderness to a fairly substantial civilization on the shores of Narragansett Bay.

Williams never lost his sharp tongue and love of argument; he once spent three days in debate with the Quakers of Providence trying to make them give up their "errors." However, he had great sympathy, as shown in this quotation written to a friend, John Winthrop, Jr., after the death of Winthrop's wife. Williams stopped at a spring he frequently visited and wrote: "Here is the spring, I say with a sigh, but where is Elizabeth? My charity answers, 'She is gone to the Eternal Spring, and Fountain of Living Waters.'"

PEOPLE OF ACCOMPLISHMENT

One of the most notable natives of Rhode Island was Nathanael Greene of Coventry. As a high-spirited young man he loved to dance, in spite of his Quaker father's whippings for this "sin." When he went into a military career, he had to leave his Quaker faith. He became a general in the Continental armies at the age of 24, and his career was probably second only to George Washington's during the Revolution. He led the campaign in the southern colonies which eventually ended in the surrender of British forces. He was only 44 when he died.

Another of Rhode Island's well-known military figures was not a native, but General Ambrose Burnside led the First Rhode Island Regiment in the Civil War. He rose to fame in that war, although with limited success in his war command. He served Rhode Island as a governor and also in the United State Senate. His name lives on in the term which describes heavy whiskers which he wore on both sides of his face. These became popular and were known as Burnsides (now incorrectly called sideburns).

One of the two greatest heroes of the War of 1812 was Oliver

Hazard Perry, who saved the country from invasion from the north by his victory at Lake Erie. From his home in Rocky Brook at South Kingstown he went to build and command his fleet. Oliver Hazard Perry was sent on a government mission to Venezuela and died there of yellow fever in 1819 at the early age of 34. His younger brother was Commodore Matthew Calbraith Perry, who is renowned for having been the first to open the ports of Japan to modern commerce.

Perry's restored flagship, Niagara, *in Erie, Pennsylvania.*

One of the most remarkable of America's great early families was the Brown family of Rhode Island. Many members of the family showed great skill and daring as merchants, manufacturers, sailors, and scientists. Among the first Rhode Island settlers was Chad Brown. His great-grandsons were James and Obadiah Brown, who owned shipping and commercial interests. When James Brown died, Obadiah kept on with the business, and he brought into it the four sons of James: Nicholas, Joseph, John, and Moses.

Joseph Brown remained in the family business only long enough to make his fortune. Then he devoted his time to the study of science, accepted a trusteeship of Rhode Island College (now Brown University) and later became a professor of science there. He was well known for his brilliance in mathematics and astronomy. However, he also was one of the best architects of early America, designer of the beautiful and highly praised First Baptist Meeting House of Providence, among many other notable buildings. Others of the Brown family formed various well-known companies. John Brown was one of the best known. Moses Brown, of course, later became known as the "father of the American textile industry."

Related to the Brown family was Pardon Tillinghast, who built the first wharf at Providence. He later became a minister and at his own expense built the first church building for the Baptists. It was a peculiar building "in the shape of a haycap, with a fireplace in the middle, the smoke escaping from a hole in the roof."

In the field of government few were more sincere or devoted than reformer Thomas Wilson Dorr, often described as "one of America's greatest champions of democracy," whose efforts resulted in personal failure and disgrace but eventually brought about a new and more liberal constitution for Rhode Island.

Another notable figure was Stephen Hopkins, ten times governor of the state, chief justice of the Superior Court, and first chancellor of Brown University. Perhaps his greatest moment came when he signed the Declaration of Independence with a noticeably shaky signature. "My hand trembles, but my heart does not," he said.

Other prominent public figures include Thomas Willett, who became the first mayor of New York and is buried in East Providence; powerful United States Senator Nelson A. Aldrich; General Charles R. Brayton, said to have been "for 30 years the Republican 'boss' of the state"; the Dyer family, which provided a father and son, both named Elisha and both governors of Rhode Island; and John Hay, secretary of state under McKinley and Roosevelt. Among the other associations of President John F. Kennedy with Rhode Island was his PT boat training at the Melville section of the Newport Naval Base.

Among recent prominent public figures was Theodore Francis Green, who was elected governor in 1932. When he retired from the U.S. Senate in 1960, at the age of 93, he was the oldest man ever to serve in the Senate.

Many scientists, inventors, and professional people are connected with Rhode Island. George H. Corliss invented a new type of steam engine which was given his name. Elijah Ormsby ran a steamboat in Narragansett Bay as early as 1796, although it did not become commercially practical. Cullen Whipple patented the first machine ever to make pointed screws. Clarence King was a famed geologist. Frank E. Seagrave was a prominent astronomer, as was Jabez Bowen. Zachariah Allen was a scientist who became a manufacturer, inventor, author, and reformer; he also found time to read law and earn a certificate in medicine.

Another medical "personality" was Sarah Sands, the first woman doctor in the English colonies, who practiced on Block Island in the 1680s and 1690s, dying there in 1702.

Peter Harrison of Newport has been called "America's first professional architect," and also "the most notable architect of Colonial America." Richard Munday, builder of Newport's second Trinity Church and the second Colony House, was another of America's fine early architects.

George William Curtis gained fame as Editor of *Harper's Weekly*, and the Reverend Samuel Newman was known as the compiler of a much-used concordance of the Bible. Captain Robert Gray of Gould Island was the first American to travel completely around the world; he is also known as the discoverer of the Columbia River on the West Coast.

Entertainment figures of Rhode Island include composer-entertainer George M. Cohan, born in Providence; singer Nelson Eddy; pianist Frankie Carle; and opera stars Eileen Farrell and Jules Jordan, who sang in premieres of works by both Berlioz and Gounod. Another Rhode Island musician was David Wallis Reeves, who has been called a "forerunner of John Philip Sousa." Motion picture personality Van Johnson is a native of Newport. Napoleon (Nap) Lajoie was the first baseball player ever named to the Baseball Hall of Fame; he gained fame as the holder of the first American League batting championship. Another Rhode Island baseball immortal was Charles L. (Gabby) Hartnett.

SUCH CREATIVE PEOPLE

Probably the best-known native of Rhode Island in the arts is Gilbert Stuart, born in North Kingstown, who became one of the world's most famous portrait painters. His father was a snuff grinder, and Gilbert was born in the home which also housed the snuff mill. As a boy he attracted attention by his fine drawings of dogs. He began to study painting at Newport, then went to Edinburgh, Scotland, for further study. In London he became known as one of the greatest portrait painters. Returning to America, he painted portraits of most of the prominent men, but of course his greatest fame rests on the many paintings he made of George Washington.

One of the best-known painters of miniatures was Edward G. Malbone; another well-known Rhode Island artist was Edward M. Bannister.

Oliver La Farge won the Pulitzer Prize in 1929 for his novel *Laughing Boy*. His *Long Pennant* is a novel dealing with Rhode Island privateers in the War of 1812. Another Rhode Island Pulitzer Prize winner (1962) is Edwin O'Connor, native of Woonsocket, for his novel *Edge of Sadness*. His earlier novel *The Last Hurrah* was a best seller and was made into a motion picture. Leonard Bacon of Peace Dale took Pulitzer honors for poetry in 1941 with his *Sunderland*

The Gilbert Stuart homestead in Saunder's Town.

Capture. Still another Rhode Island Pulitzer Prize winner, Maud Howe Elliott, received the award in 1917 for her biography of her mother, Julia Ward Howe.

The husband and wife writing team of Katya and Bert Gilden published their first novel, *Hurry Sundown,* in 1965, under the professional name of K.B. Gilden. It became one of the most popular works of its period.

Providence poetess and seeress Sarah Helen Whitman was courted by poet Edgar Allan Poe. Although they did not marry, many experts feel that Sarah Whitman was the inspiration for Poe's poems *To Helen* and *Annabel Lee.* The engagement was ended because her family did not approve of Poe.

SUCH INTERESTING PEOPLE

Among the many interesting women of Rhode Island were the society leaders who helped make Newport one of the world's great social centers. One of the most prominent of these was Mrs. William Astor, who is said to have "reigned at Newport." Others were Mrs. Stuyvesant Fish, Mrs. Pembroke Jones, Mrs. Oliver Belmont, and Mrs. Cornelius Vanderbilt.

Right: An aerial view of the Vanderbilt mansion at Newport. Below: The front of Marble House.

*The ballroom
in Marble House.*

More adventurous were Annie S. Peck, who climbed a mountain in Peru (the peak was named in her honor), and Idawalley Zorada Lewis of Newport. Daughter of a lighthouse keeper in Newport Harbor, she gained international fame by her rescues of drowning persons. She received mail from all over the world, and President Ulysses S. Grant visited her at the lighthouse on Lime Rock. She was made keeper of the light in 1899. The United States government gave her a gold lifesaving medal; people danced to the Ida Lewis Waltz; even scarves and garments were named in her honor, as was the lighthouse, at a later date.

Daring in her own way was Aunt Susie Smith of Warren who fought, kicked, bit, and scratched two British soldiers in 1778 to save the family silver.

At twelve years of age Betsey Metcalf of Providence in 1798 introduced the weaving of straw hats into this country.

The second wife of Brigham Young, Mary Ann Angell, was born at Providence in 1804. She enjoyed great respect of the members of the Mormon faith, and now is known as "Mother Young."

William Ellery Channing, "Apostle of Unitarianism," was born at Newport. Another prominent religious leader was Rabbi Judah

Touro, who gave land around the Old Stone Mill to the city of Newport. He made his fortune in New Orleans and helped Andrew Jackson when he defended that city in the War of 1812. On his death, Rabbi Touro left an estate of $500,000 to churches of many faiths and to other institutions.

One of the unique personalities associated with Rhode Island was cunning Sachem Ninigret of the Niantic, one of the few Indian leaders of his period who did not meet a violent death. At one time he is said to have told an English missionary to convert the English first before he came to the Indians.

Another personality was Joseph Brown Ladd, native of Newport, who at 22 was already a poet of stature when he was killed in a duel. At the age of 10 he began to publish his satires on prominent people.

Others include James De Wolfe, fabulous privateer on his ship *Yankee;* the Reverend Obadiah Holmes, who established the second Baptist society in America in 1644 and who was an ancestor of Abraham Lincoln; eccentric weaver William Harrison Rose, who did much to reestablish hand weaving in America; Axel de Ferson of Providence, who is said never to have smiled after Marie Antoinette was executed; and Pero Bonnister, whose nose was so long and his casket so shallow that a hole had to be cut in the casket, and he was buried with his nose sticking through.

One of the most prominent Newport residents during the city's reign as social center of the country was Harry Lehr, known as the "Joker of Newport." He often helped Mrs. William Astor with her guest lists, but he could not refrain from playing jokes such as elaborate hoaxes on Newport society. It was said that Mrs. Astor was the queen and Lehr was her jester. He was noted also for his unusual and ingenious party themes and novelties. At one elaborate "social" affair he invited about a hundred of the "best" dogs of Newport, who could bring their masters. One of the dachshunds ate so much it collapsed and had to be escorted home. On another occasion Lehr and Mrs. Stuyvesant Fish invited guests to a sumptuous party to meet the "Prince del Drago." The guest of honor turned out to be a small monkey, elaborately clothed in the finest full-dress suit of the day.

Teaching and Learning

The best-known educational institution of Rhode Island is Brown University—seventh oldest of America's higher education institutions. It was chartered in 1764 as Rhode Island College, first located at Warren. Its charter stated: "Into this Liberal and Catholic (universal) Institution shall never be admitted any religious Tests but on the Contrary all the Members hereof shall forever enjoy full free Absolute and uninterrupted Liberty of Conscience."

The college held its first commencement in 1769. It is interesting to note that students were unruly even in those days. After a later commencement, a committee asked the general assembly to "authorize and direct the Sheriff . . . to attend on this corporation on Commencement days, in future and by himself or deputies, to preserve the peace, good order, and decorum . . . that it be recommended to the Baptist Society, in future, to take effectual measures to prevent the erection of Booths, or receptacles for liquors . . . and other disorderly practices on the Baptist Meeting-House lot."

An unusual contest was held to decide the final location of the college: "Some who were unwilling it should be there in Warren and some who were unwilling it should be anywhere, did so far agree as to lay aside the said location and purpose that the county which should raise the most money should have the college." Providence won this contest over Newport, the next highest bidder, and the college was moved to Providence in 1770. Because of the generosity of Nicholas Brown, it was named Brown University in 1804.

Among many memorable dates in the university's history were 1770 when University Hall (now a national historic landmark) was built, 1790 when George Washington received an honorary degree, and 1926 when the renowned Iron Men football team had a tremendously successful year, defeating both Yale and Dartmouth.

Women undergraduates were enrolled in a separate college, Pembroke College, established in 1892 as the Women's College in Brown University.

Among the distinctions of the university, probably the most notable is John Carter Brown Library, which has among its many groups of books a collection of Americana said to be the "finest in the world." The John Hay library also has notable collections, including one on Lincoln called the "most complete in the world."

The University of Rhode Island at Kingston was begun in 1892 as Rhode Island College, a land-grant institution. It was named the University of Rhode Island in 1951, and is one of the most recent of all the state universities to be named. There are seven main divisions of the university. One of its early distinctions was teaching the first complete course ever given in poultry husbandry. One of the interesting educational efforts of the university is the Graduate School of Oceanography, another is the Bureau of Government Research; there is also a Water Resources Research Center.

Rhode Island College at Providence began in 1854 as the Rhode Island Normal School, and later as the Rhode Island College of Education. It still specializes in education, although other courses are offered.

One of the outstanding institutions of its type is the Rhode Island School of Design at Providence, incorporated in 1877; it offers courses in fine arts, architecture, landscape architecture, and art education. The school maintains a center in Rome, Italy, for future professional designers, who spend a year studying with European experts in their fields.

Another widely recognized specialized school is Bryant College, once located at Providence, but now in Smithfield.

It was begun in 1863 for liberal and business education; today its major divisions are the school of business administration, business teacher education, and the school of secretarial science.

Providence College was founded in 1917 by the Most Reverend Matthew Harkins, with its faculty mostly drawn from the Dominican order. A Catholic school for women is Salve Regina College, The Newport College, Newport.

Other Rhode Island colleges include Barrington College, Barrington, and Roger Williams College, Bristol.

A novel higher education institution is the Naval War College at Newport, founded in 1884 by Admiral Stephen B. Luce. Top experts from all the service and government departments arrive almost daily

Salve Regina, the Newport College, founded in 1947.

to lecture the 300 naval officers of middle and senior rank who take refresher courses there.

Robert Lenthal came to Newport in 1640 "to keep a public school for learning of the youth." Although it may not have continued for long, this is thought to have been the first school in Rhode Island. Other schools were established during the 1600s and early 1700s. It is interesting to note that between 1760 and 1830 schools depended mainly on income from lotteries. The first free public school law was established in 1800; Providence began to set up public schools after that time. By 1823 there was at least one schoolhouse in each town.

Rhode Island's present school system is considered to have begun with the passage of the Barnard school law of 1845. A state board of education was founded in 1870, and by that year Rhode Island had six public high schools as well as many private academies. Among the prominent private schools of the state are St. George's School and Portsmouth Abbey School, both near Portsmouth.

Leading American educators from Rhode Island have included Mary C. Wheeler and Francis Wayland, an educational reformer who was known as the foremost educator of his time. "He devoted his whole secular life to making education available to the ordinary American citizen." Among many accomplishments, he was one of the first to propose the elective system in college education.

The skyline of Providence.

Enchantment of Rhode Island

"Rhode Island has more to offer the summer vacationer than any other area of comparable size in the United States," asserted the New York *Herald Tribune*. The attractions have inspired 17 Presidents to vacation in the state, as well as millions of others. There are historic cities and towns dating back to the 1600s, offering some of the nation's finest examples of early American architecture. The sports attractions are some of the best sailing waters in the world, some of the finest beaches, state piers for fishing, state parks and areas, and Narragansett Park racetrack. In winter there is skiing, "frostbite sailing," and curling.

Cultural activities encouraged by the Rhode Island Fine Arts Council include two philharmonic orchestras, but the Rhode Island Arts Festival and the Newport Jazz Festival have been discontinued.

People go to Rhode Island for the famous clambakes, which the Indians taught the early settlers, and for Rhode Island clam chowder and Rhode Island johnnycake and many other good foods. Johnny-cake was originally known as journey-cake, because it could be made easily on long trips. It is said to be called johnnycake in honor of Governor Jonathan Trumbull.

GOD'S MERCIFUL PROVIDENCE

"Having of a sense of God's merciful providence unto me called this place Providence, I desired it might be for a shelter for persons distressed for conscience," wrote Roger Williams as he named, in honor of God, the city that someday would be the second largest in New England. Modern visitors are interested to see that streets still carry out the city's theme with such names as Peace, Faith, Friendship, Benefit, Benevolent, and Hope.

The city's long and colorful history is composed of such diverse and long-separated events as the establishment by John Smith in 1646 of Rhode Island's first gristmill, the paving of Providence streets in 1761 with funds gained from a lottery, and the protection of the city from floods by the completion of Fox Point Dam as a hurricane barrier in 1961.

The Civic Center, Exchange Place, is said to be the first and one of the finest central squares of its kind in the country. Today its outstanding feature is the Industrial Trust Building, topped by a huge lantern, an outstanding landmark of Providence. The nation's first shopping center was the Arcade Building; its columns are believed to be the largest monoliths in the country, except for those of New York's Cathedral of St. John the Divine. Another early commercial enterprise is Gladding's, which claims to be the oldest department store in America.

Providence also asserts that the Crawford Street Bridge is the widest in the world, composed of six units totaling 1,147 feet (350 meters) in width.

One of the outstanding public buildings in America is the Rhode Island capitol, for which ground was broken in 1895; the cornerstone was laid in 1896 and the statehouse was occupied in 1900. Perhaps an even more significant date was 1941, when the last bonds were burned to celebrate the final payment on the building's debt. This "marble palace," containing about 327,000 cubic feet (9,260 cubic meters) of white Georgia marble, has the world's second largest unsupported marble dome, next in size to the dome of St. Peter's in Italy and largest of its type in the United States. The only other such marble domes existing in the world are the Taj Mahal in India and the capitol at St. Paul, Minnesota. The total cost of the Rhode Island capitol was $3,018,416.33.

At the top of the dome is a statue known as *The Independent Man*. Roger Williams' statue was supposed to have been placed there, but the capitol architect, Charles McKim, pointed out that no likeness of Williams had been passed down to the present day. The figure caused considerable controversy, but now the "man" is well liked, as a symbol of Rhode Island's independent people. In 1927 he was struck by lightning and 42 copper "stitches" had to be taken to repair the damage.

One of the most precious artistic possessions of the state is the portrait of George Washington by Gilbert Stuart in the capitol. Many

"The Independent Man" stands atop the capitol.

paintings—of Ambrose Burnside and other historic figures—hang in Memorial Hall on the second floor. The interior of the dome has a huge mural 50 feet (15 meters) across, which shows the history of the state. A prize historical relic, housed in the office of the secretary of state, is the original parchment charter granted by Charles II, July 8, 1663.

The old statehouse, used from 1762 until 1900, where Rhode Island's freedom was proclaimed, is still a public building. Another massive building of the capital city is the Providence County Courthouse, dedicated in 1933 at a total cost of $4,592,428.68.

Among the best-known buildings in New England is the First Baptist Meeting House of Providence, built in 1775 for the oldest Baptist society in America. The First Unitarian Church boasts the largest bell ever cast by Paul Revere.

President John Adams called the John Brown House "the finest mansion in America." Beautifully preserved, it is now headquarters of the Rhode Island Historical Society, with a museum of early furnishings.

Roger Williams Park of Providence has been called "one of the most beautiful municipal parks in the country." Others go so far as to say it is the "greatest in the world!" The park was willed to the city in 1871 by Betsey Williams, great-great-granddaughter of Roger Williams. Her modest home may still be seen in the park. The park itself is a beautifully cared for arboretum of more than 300 species of woody plants, native and foreign.

A $1,300,000 conservatory donated by Charles H. Smith is one of the newest features of Roger Williams Park, which also has an outstanding zoo. The Benedict Temple of Music, nestled in a valley near Cunliff Lake, provides a Grecian setting for musical and dramatic productions. The park museum houses natural history collections. There is also a planetarium and museum.

An outstanding institution is the Museum of Art of the Rhode Island School of Design, often called "one of the nation's most distinguished small museums." Providence Art Club also has a gallery of art.

Historic Benefit Street in Providence.

One of the city's principal cultural institutions is its library, the Providence Athenaeum, among the oldest libraries in the country. Here Edgar Allan Poe and his Helen (Whitman) used to meet.

NEWPORT

Few cities in America have a history as rich and varied and colorful as that of Newport, and a still smaller number of cities can display so many great examples from the past still in existence.

Newport is really three different towns in one: the seaport and business center; Naval Base and Naval War College; and the summer colony, not so brilliant as it once was but still maintaining much social distinction.

Even before the Revolutionary War, Newport was a center of society and culture, the first summer resort in America. Wealthy and prominent people from the south began to come to Newport for the summer in the 1750s. The first lectures ever given in America on dentistry and medicine were offered at Newport in 1756. New England's first professional dramatic performance was given at Newport on September 7, 1761. By 1769 Newport was one of the leading cities of the colonies, said to be "well ahead" of New York.

Among its many distinctions, Newport can boast of the oldest continuously operated business in the nation—the John Stevens stonecutting shop, the first Masonic lodge in America, the first street in America to be lit with gas (1806), the oldest artillery company in North America, and the first national championships in golf and tennis.

One of the great charms of Newport is that much of it has remained almost identical to the community of 200 years ago. One of the principal forces in keeping and restoring the city's historic face is the Preservation Society of Newport County.

One of Newport's most famous buildings is Touro Synagogue, built in 1763 for Congregation Yeshuat Israel, now a national historic site and the oldest synagogue in America. In addition to historic features, it is noted as one of the best designed buildings of

Right: The Chateau Sur Mer in Newport. Below: The Newport Bridge.

*The America's Cup
sailing races
off Newport.*

its period. Newport's Jewish population dates from about 1658. In 1822, Abraham Touro left $10,000 as a perpetual bequest to maintain "Touro Jewish Synagogue." Judah Touro, a brother of Abraham, left another $10,000 for services and care of the synagogue.

In 1790, President George Washington wrote a letter to the Newport Jewish congregation which was one of his most interesting comments on the subject of religion: ". . . the Government of the United States, which gives to bigotry no sanction, to persecution no assistance, requires only that they who live under its protection should demean themselves as good citizens, in giving it on all occasions their effectual support . . . . May the Children of the Stock of Abraham, who dwell in this land, continue to merit and enjoy the good will of the other Inhabitants; while everyone shall sit in safety under his own vine and figtree . . . . May the father of all mercies scatter light and not darkness in our paths, and make us all in our several vocations useful here, and in his own due time and way everlastingly happy."

Another Newport national historic landmark is Rhode Island's second capitol building, the Old Colony House, on what is now the northerly end of Washington Square. It is considered to be the second oldest capitol building in the United States.

The mansions of the wealthy at Newport are probably the best-known modern feature of the city. Most famous of these was The Breakers, built by Cornelius Vanderbilt in 1895 for $3,000,000 and made to resemble an Italian palace. It contains about 70 rooms; the elaborate ornamentation and furnishings are a major feature of the building, which Vanderbilt called a "cottage." The building is now open to the public. The carriage house and stable of The Breakers is now one of the finest museums of carriages and other horse-drawn equipment.

Marble House, one of the most sumptuous of Newport's "cottages," was completed in 1892 for William K. Vanderbilt. It takes its name from the many kinds of marble used in its construction. The most elaborate room in the house is the ballroom, known as the Gold Room. It is also open to the public.

One of the most beautiful French chateaus in America is The Elms, built in 1901 as the summer residence of Edward J. Berwind, Philadelphia coal magnate. The mansion is completely furnished with outstanding museum pieces, some part of the original furnishings, others lent by museums and private collectors. The whole house is ablaze with lights when it is open on Saturday evening. The grounds are among the most beautiful in Newport.

Famous Ocean Drive and Bellevue Avenue show an imposing array of millionaires' mansions.

Over the region broods the memory of the famous and would-be-famous people who flocked to Newport when a summer in Newport was more socially desirable than a summer in Europe. These were the gilded years of Newport. Entertaining was done on a magnificent scale. Mrs. Fish and Mrs. Goelet battled (with social weapons, not fists) for the Grand Duke of Russia. Mrs. Cornelius Vanderbilt taught him to play golf, which he then introduced to Russia. There are memories of all the opulence and splendor and often of the unhappiness which seemed to go with such "high" social life.

Today Newport's activities are open to a much wider circle. One of the famous celebrations of music at Newport, the Folk Music Festival and Jazz Festival over the Fourth of July, attracted so many thousands that riots occurred in earlier years.

Other activities are Tennis Week at the Newport Casino, a tour of Newport Mansions in August, and the Bermuda Race, in which racing yachts start at Newport over a 635-mile (1,022-kilometer) course to Bermuda.

One of the principal work activities of Newport is connected with the Naval Education and Training Center.

OTHER POINTS OF INTEREST

Woonsocket is the most northerly metropolitan center of Rhode Island, with its entire northern boundary touching the Massachusetts line. Many visitors are struck by the French quality of the city, due to the large numbers of French Canadian people there. Most speak both French and English, but French is often heard throughout the city.

The city had its beginning in a sawmill built by Richard Arnold on the Blackstone River in 1666. No other buildings were constructed until about thirty years had passed. The community grew slowly during the 1700s, but owed its greatest growth to the textile industry, begun in 1810 by the Ballou brothers (Ariel, Abner, and Nathan), Luke and Job Jenckes, Eben Bartlett, and Joseph Arnold. They formed the Social Manufacturing Company and built a small mill. Cotton textiles formed the basis of the Woonsocket industry until 1901, when woolen yarns and fabrics took the lead. The woolen industry had been started in 1840 by Edward Harris.

Today Woonsocket is a manufacturing center with diversified industries. Nearby Diamond Hill State Park offers ski slopes and tows, a toboggan run, skating pond, and other attractions both winter and summer.

The Indian word *Pawtucket* means "at the falls." The first settler at the falls was Joseph Jencks, Jr., in 1671. The falls that gave the city its name furnished power for the old Slater Mill, now completely and lovingly restored as a monument to America's industrial heritage, the birthplace of American industry. Here was the first successful textile mill in America, and it heralded the rapid and later unequaled expansion of manufacturing that made the country the world's leading industrial nation. The old mill now also houses a museum of early industry.

Another Pawtucket building of interest is the Daggett House, built in 1685 and furnished in its period.

Narragansett Park (a racetrack near Pawtucket) is a different kind of attraction, which brings many horse lovers to the Pawtucket area.

Warren was the home of one of the great Indian friends of the Europeans—Chief Massasoit. Cranston is a residential and industrial suburb of Providence, having almost 100 industries. One of the most interesting of these is the Cranston Print Works Company where visitors may see the interesting processes used in printing cloth.

An art show in Narragansett.

*Rhode Island Reds; only
Rhode Island has such
a practical state bird.*

Nearby Bristol remembers the original inhabitants in its Haffenreffer Museum of the American Indian, housing one of the nation's most comprehensive collections of Indian relics, as well as those of Eskimos. Hope Street in Bristol is a famous row of well-preserved colonial homes. The widows of Bristol probably hope for the restoration of an old town law which required the minister, John Usher, to care for all the widows of the parish out of his salary. A well-known resident of Bristol was John Brown Herreshoff, the blind designer of famous racing yachts.

At Tiverton is one of the nation's few monuments to the animal kingdom—the Red Hen Monument—honoring the state's poultry product.

On the island of Conanicut (Jamestown) is the oldest YWCA summer camp in the country. An old windmill has been restored by the Jamestown Historical Society.

Block Island has been called Rhode Island's "naturally air-conditioned summer resort" because it is cooler than the mainland. The island has no skunks or snakes. The famed spring and fall migrations of birds attract many to Block Island.

Two shrines to famous men are particularly well known in the state. The artist Gilbert Stuart's birthplace is now restored as the snuff mill that it was in the youth of the great portraitist. The Nathanael Greene birthplace near Anthony is sometimes known as the "Mount Vernon of New England."

Colt Farm in Bristol.

The village of Wickford is renowned as the location of more fine old houses than any other community of its size in New England.

East Greenwich made its contribution to textile history by being the site of the country's first calico printing. Today one of the attractions of the region is the New England Museum of Wireless and Radio at East Greenwich. Also at East Greenwich is the General James Mitchell Varnum House and Museum, home of the Revolutionary officer and lawyer.

One of the major natural attractions of the state is Stepstone Falls in West Greenwich. Among the other outstanding falls of Rhode Island is picturesque Horseshoe Falls near Shannock. Another natural feature is the Talking Rock at Apponaug. At one time the rock would make a booming noise if moved slightly back and forth. Unfortunately, it has been silent for some time.

One of the major fishing events of the country is the Atlantic Tuna Tournament held at the port of Galilee each year.

Davisville is the original home of the United States Naval Construction Center, better known as headquarters of the famous Seabees. Nearby was Quonset Point Naval Air Station. The word quonset comes from the Indian name *seconiqueonset,* which means a neck of land. The prefabricated quonset hut developed there by the Navy during World War II was named for nearby Quonset Point, and the squat prefabricated building has carried the name around the world.

Small as it is, Rhode Island has managed to merit such world attention in a surprising list of accomplishments.

Handy Reference Section

Instant Facts

Became the 13th state, May 29, 1790
Official name—State of Rhode Island and Providence Plantations
Nickname—Little Rhody or The Ocean State
Capital—Providence, settled 1636
State motto—Hope
State bird—Rhode Island Red chicken
State tree—Red maple
State flower—Violet (unofficial)
State rock—Cumberlandite
State song—"Rhode Island"
Area—1,214 square miles (3,144 square kilometers)
Rank in area—50th
Shoreline—384 miles (618 kilometers)
Greatest length (north to south)—48 miles (77 kilometers)
Greatest width (east to west)—37 miles (60 kilometers)
Geographic center—Kent, 1 mile (1.6 kilometers) south southwest of Crompton
Highest point—812 feet (247 meters), Jerimoth Hill
Lowest point—Sea level
Number of counties—5
Population—1,027,000 (1980 projection)
Rank in population—39th
Population density—846 persons per square mile (327 persons per square kilometer)
Rank in density—2nd
Population center—In Cranston City, Providence County, 5.5 miles (9 kilometers) south of Providence
Birthrate—12.6 per 1,000
Infant mortality rate—17.3 per 1,000 births
Physicians per 100,000—173

Principal cities—	Providence	179,116	(1970 census)
	Warwick	83,694	
	Pawtucket	76,894	
	Cranston	74,287	
	East Providence	48,207	
	Woonsocket	46,820	
	Newport	34,562	

You Have a Date with History

1524—Verrazano explores in area
1635—William Blackstone settles in area

1636 — Roger Williams begins Providence and Rhode Island
1638 — Portsmouth founded
1639 — Newport founded
1640 — First school established, Newport
1643 — Roger Williams brings "The Incorporation"
1646 — First gristmill begins
1658 — Jewish people begin to arrive
1663 — Rhode Island charter granted, basic law for 180 years
1666 — Woonsocket begins
1671 — Pawtucket founded
1675 — King Philip's War
1723 — Danger of piracy lessened by hanging of 26 pirates
1728 — Boundary with Conneticut finally settled
1732 — First newspaper published
1763 — Wars with France end; Touro Synagogue built at Newport
1764 — Beginnings of present Brown University
1765 — Newport men burn the British ship *Maidstone*
1769 — Brown, Bowen and Hopkins observe transit of Venus
1772 — Gaspee incident, in which British ship *Gaspee* was burned by patriots
1775 — First Baptist Meeting House built at Providence
1776 — Rhode Island becomes first independent republic of New World; Newport occupied
1778 — Battle of Rhode Island
1779 — Newport evacuated by British
1784 — Slavery abolished
1790 — Statehood; dawn of America's Industrial Revolution when first cotton factory opens at Pawtucket
1815 — Power looms introduced
1817 — Steamboat navigation begins
1835 — First steam railroad
1842 — Dorr Rebellion forces new constitution
1845 — Modern state school system begins
1854 — Rhode Island Red chicken first bred
1861 — Civil War begins; 24,000 from Rhode Island serve, 1,520 die
1871 — Betsey Williams leaves Roger Williams Park to Providence
1880 — Rhode Island becomes the leading jewelry producing state
1892 — Beginning of the University of Rhode Island
1895 — Cornelius Vanderbilt finishes The Breakers
1898 — Spanish American War; 3,246 from Rhode Island serve
1900 — Providence made sole capital; present capitol occupied
1917 — World War I begins; 28,817 from Rhode Island serve; 684 die
1922 — Textile strike begins, spreads over New England
1929 — First state airport in country authorized
1930 — Newport has its first America's Cup race
1933 — Providence County Courthouse dedicated
1936 — 300th Anniversary of Rhode Island founding celebrated; prehistoric Folsom Point discovered, East Providence

90

1938—Hurricane becomes worst natural disaster in state's history
1941—World War II begins; 92,027 from Rhode Island serve; 1,458 die
1954—Rhode Island Red made state bird
1959—First state sponsored opera in United States
1960—First fully automated post office in the United States opened at Providence
1966—Republicans sweep three top elected posts for first time since 1938
1969—Newport Bridge over Narragansett Bay completed
1976—Bicentennial celebration includes a welcome to the "Tall Ships"

Governors of Rhode Island (since statehood)

Arthur Fenner 1790-1805	John W. Davis 1887-1888
Henry Smith 1805	Royal C. Taft 1888-1889
Isaac Wilbur 1806-1807	Herbert W. Ladd 1889-1890
James Fenner 1807-1811	John W. Davis 1890-1891
William Jones 1811-1817	Herbert W. Ladd 1891-1892
Nehemiah R. Knight 1817-1821	D. Russell Brown 1892-1895
William C. Gibbs 1821-1824	Charles Warren Lippitt 1895-1897
James Fenner 1824-1831	Elisha Dyer 1897-1900
Lemuel H. Arnold 1831-1833	William Gregory 1900-1901
John Brown Francis 1833-1838	Charles Dean Kimball 1901-1903
William Sprague 1838-1839	Lucius F.C. Garvin 1903-1905
Samuel Ward King 1840-1843	George H. Utter 1905-1907
James Fenner 1843-1845	James H. Higgins 1907-1909
Charles Jackson 1845-1846	Aram J. Pothier 1909-1915
Byron Diman 1846-1847	R. Livingston Beeckman 1915-1921
Elisha Harris 1847-1849	Emery J. San Souci 1921-1923
Henry B. Anthony 1849-1851	William S. Flynn 1923-1925
Philip Allen 1851-1853	Aram J. Pothier 1925-1928
Francis M. Dimond 1853-1854	Norman S. Case 1928-1933
William Warner Hoppin 1854-1857	Theodore Francis Green 1933-1937
Elisha Dyer 1857-1859	Robert E. Quinn 1937-1939
Thomas G. Turner 1859-1860	William H. Vanderbilt 1939-1941
William Sprague 1860-1863	J. Howard McGrath 1941-1945
William C. Cozzens 1863	John O. Pastore 1945-1950
James Y. Smith 1863-1866	John S. McKiernan 1950-1951
Ambrose E. Burnside 1866-1869	Dennis J. Roberts 1951-1959
Seth Padelford 1869-1873	Christopher Del Sesto 1959-1961
Henry Howard 1873-1875	John A. Notte, Jr. 1961-1963
Henry Lippitt 1875-1877	John H. Chafee 1963-1969
Charles C. Van Zandt 1877-1880	Frank Licht 1969-1973
Alfred H. Littlefield 1880-1883	Philip W. Noel 1973-1977
Augustus O. Bourn 1883-1885	J. Joseph Garrahy 1977-
George Peabody Wetmore 1885-1887	

Index

92

93

PICTURE CREDITS

ABOUT THE AUTHOR

With the publication of his first book for school use when he was twenty, **Allan Carpenter** began a career as an author that has spanned more than 135 books. After teaching in the public schools of Des Moines, Mr. Carpenter began his career as an educational publisher at the age of twenty-one when he founded the magazine *Teachers Digest.* In the field of educational periodicals, he was responsible for many innovations. During his many years in publishing, he has perfected a highly organized approach to handling large volumes of factual material: after extensive traveling and having collected all possible materials, he systematically reviews and organizes everything. From his apartment high in Chicago's John Hancock Building, Allan recalls, "My collection and assimilation of materials on the states and countries began before the publication of my first book." Allan is the founder of Carpenter Publishing House and of Infordata International, Inc., publishers of *Issues in Education* and *Index to U. S. Government Periodicals.* When he is not writing or traveling, his principal avocation is music. He has been the principal bassist of many symphonies, and he managed the country's leading non-professional symphony for twenty-five years.